An Experiment in Living

~

SHARING A HOUSE IN LATER LIFE

Acknowledgments

Thanks to our families and the friends who have indulged us during endless discussions about this book!

AN EXPERIMENT IN LIVING
~

SHARING A HOUSE IN LATER LIFE

June Green
Jenny Betts
Greta Wilson

Illustrations by Maggie Guillon

Third Age Press
London 1999

Third Age Press

ISBN 1 898576 14 9
First edition

Third Age Press Ltd, 1999
Third Age Press, 6 Parkside Gardens
London SW19 5EY
Managing Editor Dianne Norton

© Jenny Betts, June Green, Greta Wilson

Illustrations © by Maggie Guillon
Cover design by Sam Hill

All rights reserved. This book is sold subject to the condition that it shall not, by way of trade or otherwise, be lent, re-sold, hired out or otherwise circulated without the publisher's prior consent in any form of binding or cover other than that in which it is published and without a similar condition including this condition being imposed on the subsequent purchaser.

Layout design by Dianne Norton
Printed and bound in Great Britain
by Intype

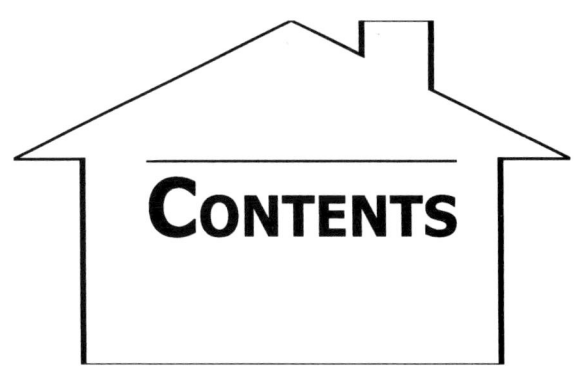

Introduction 8
Points to ponder 13
Do you really want to share a house? 20
What's in it for you?
What are you prepared to give up?
Do you know other people who are interested?
Would you need to know people really well in order to share with them?
Are you prepared to spend a lot of time discussing the basic idea, difficulties, areas of concern – e.g. telephones, diet, money, family needs, personal space, possible differences in income, etc. etc. etc!

A question of space – or how to choose a house 26
Where do you want to live – town or country?
Do you all agree?
What are the most important factors for you?
How much shared space do you anticipate having?
Do you want/can you afford a house allowing for separate kitchen/living space/en suite facilities?
How much work are you prepared to have done to make a potentially acceptable house into what you really want? Can you afford it?
What are your criteria for allocating rooms?

Buying the house – legal and financial questions   **35**
How much can you afford to pay for a house?
What are your present outgoings? Will it cost more? Can you afford it?
Can you agree on a price range for a house?
Do you need a mortgage? What if anyone involved does not?
Do you have a good and sympathetic solicitor?
Have you thought about how necessary legal arrangements may affect your will?
Have you thought about the implications of future illness or infirmity?
How does your family feel about arrangements that will need to be made?

Making the move   **45**
Problems of synchronising sales of existing properties.
What furniture is needed? What kitchen appliances/utensils/crockery etc?
Tying up all the legal points.
Moving in without falling over each other!
Deciding how to arrange it all. Where shall we keep the salt/bread/etc?!
Whose furniture goes where?

Settling in   **50**
Sorting out administration
Who does the shopping? When?
How are weekly/monthly expenses dealt with?
Who does the cooking? Who decides what to eat?
Housework – how much, when, who does it?
Priorities?
Household jobs generally – gardening, cleaning out the drains?

Washing – do you need a rota?
Television – who watches what, and where?
Transition – making changes?

Transition - making changes?   59
Redefining the spaces
Dealing with possible disagreements about change
How tolerant/flexible are you really?

Options - alternative ways to share   63
Cynthia Thompson's piece   69

What's in it for us?   74
June's thoughts   75
Greta's thoughts   78
Jenny's thoughts   81
A short tale from our fourth inhabitant   85
Shirley's piece   87
From the younger generation   91

Retirement - Personal Reflections   96
Jenny's story   97
June's thoughts   100
Greta's tale   102

Sharing a house keeps us healthy   106

Postscript - *Serious stuff! (Well, most of it!)*   109

Appendix A   Questionnaire   115
Appendix B   Book list – suggested reading   117
Appendix C   Ground floor plans of both houses   119
Useful contacts   120
More about Third Age Press   123

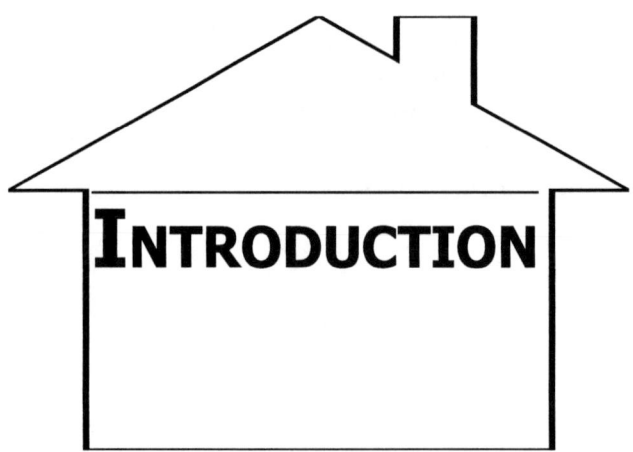

INTRODUCTION

Once upon a time there were three women, whose names were June, Greta and Jenny, and they had some very bright ideas about sharing a house, which is what this book is about. After years of doing the expected they decided to do the unexpected and, in the absence of a fairy godmother, 'do-it-yourself' seemed to be the name of the game.(And as you will see, DIY is still decidedly on-going!)

So who are these three intrepid heroines?

June is – highly verbal, interested in everything, computer literate (most of the time!), cognitively nocturnal, allergic to exercise, boringly efficient, shopping-list compiler extraordinaire, crossword puzzle addict, has Buddhist tendencies (will not kill those snails – drat her!), plant addict, medicinal sherry drinker.

Greta is – absent-minded (with honours! – where are my glasses?), theoretical DIY addict, intrepid walker, reluctant cyclist, almost illiterate map reader, whirlwind spring cleaner, budding archaeologist, organic purist, real ale drinker, serious photographer.

An experiment in living

Jenny is - addicted to change, spontaneous, a mistress of wit and repartee, intermittent wood-carver, ideas enthusiast, recipe addict, energetic gardener, wine connoisseur, totally computer illiterate, charmingly imperious!

So, we may be very different but what do we have in common? Well, we all have a keen sense of the ridiculous. We share an interest in many issues – philosophical, environmental, political, etc. We read a lot; we enjoy entertaining our children. We love living in this beautiful area to which we all chose to retire. Music, theatre, art galleries are important to all of us, and what fun that there's nearly always at least one other to share the enjoyment of these activities. These are some of the reasons which helped us to decide to take the plunge, and embark on our 'experiment'.

Of course, sharing a house in later life is not for everybody but it is one way of dealing with housing for the retired. This book is intended as a reasonably light-hearted exploration of just such a venture, one not lightly entered into but intended to make life more interesting and, hopefully, more fun. We hope that the three of us who have stayed the course and are still here, still speaking – well, most of the time! – and still enjoying the challenge, have managed to be reasonably honest. We have tried to explore the downs as well as the ups. As you will see, however many snags, problems, difficulties you anticipate there are always going to be the ones you never even dreamt of.

With a growing population of older people and greater life expectancy there is surely a need for society generally to consider fresh ways of dealing with the later years of life. Not all pensioners fit the American prosperous 'grey panther' image. Women facing retirement alone, for whatever reason, may find incomes drastically reduced. Sheltered housing, granny flats, Housing Association complexes can all provide very acceptable answers for some, but the right level of accommodation may not be easily affordable. We all examined some of the alternatives before making the decision to embark on sharing a house.

It is actually quite difficult to find out how interested people really are in the idea of a 'shared roof'. Early general discussion amongst a group of friends had led us to believe that there was a lot of enthusiasm for the idea. Not so! When two of us suggested that we look at the idea seriously, interest evaporated like soap bubbles. More to the point, there was an air of distinct hostility – some people were clearly threatened by this kind of venture. Why? Well, some of the answers will emerge in general discussion, the rest we'll try and deal with at the end.

So what's the first step, assuming that at least two of you are interested? Basically, the first things you must work out are finance, finance, and finance! How much can you afford to put into a house? What size of house can you afford to support? Do you envisage a fifty/fifty (or other equal share) in the house? Is there a great discrepancy in incomes – does one of you favour a more extravagant/frugal style of living than the other(s)? Only when you have come to some understanding on these points can you progress to the next step - where do you want to live and what kind of house do you want? Believe us when we say that you will stand or fall on these matters, and it's no good being polite. The moment to tell your prospective house mate(s) that you can't stand three-storied houses, or that bungalows give you claustrophobia is not when she/they are waxing lyrical about having found the house of their dreams and you can't wait to get out of it.

Two of us actually bought and shared the first house. We started out by drawing up lists, endless lists; we wrote down our personal requirements, we checked them with each other, kept diaries detailing both our worries and our progress in making decisions, discussed our doubts and concerns. We got out maps and studied locations. We awarded points to the houses we looked at, and discarded anything that didn't score at least 75%; above all, we looked at a lot of houses. And we still got it wrong! It was a lovely house, it was in a wonderful location, but it wasn't really big enough, or at any rate the spaces weren't in the right places. Because we had got a lot of other things right we survived – with some difficulties – but we learnt a hard lesson - never, never compromise on the house. It must be acceptable to all those involved and this may mean looking at other people's needs as well as your own.

Families have definite ideas about what mothers should and shouldn't do! Nobody's suggesting that you need permission, but if they are used to seeing a lot of you think about how you will entertain them in a shared house. Consider, too, whether you are used to having a lot of visitors to stay. Does a guest room figure on everybody's agenda? Is it going to move you too far up the price range you've settled for?

If all this thinking and planning hasn't put you off, it's time to look at the next hurdle, and this one is almost as important as the first. Do you have the right kind of solicitor? You may have an excellent one already, but he or she may not necessarily be the right person. What you need is someone sympathetic to the idea of shared roofs. Next, he or she should be prepared to go through the whole procedure with you, in minute detail. We spent one of the most gruelling hours imaginable with ours. He asked us questions we hadn't even vaguely formulated and posed hypothetical questions we'd never even imagined. Then he was kind enough to say that we had put a lot more effort into our planning than most people, and why didn't we go away and find our house. So we did. We'll explore some of these points and the legal niceties in more detail in a later section.

If two people choosing a house is difficult then when it came to four, the second time around, it was probably more than doubly hard. We were fortunate that a house of the right size and in the right location fell into our laps almost accidentally; even luckier that we all liked it. To complicate matters, by the end of the first year we were down to three and feeling very grateful to our solicitor for having been so insistent on the right kind of Trust Deed. Within six months, family circumstances had changed considerably for our fourth member and she felt that she had to return to her original home town. There were no hard feelings and it all served to make us aware that nothing is certain in this life!

Undoing her part of the arrangements proved not unduly difficult, given good will all round and properly constituted legal arrangements. Fortunately, we were able to cope with the necessary financial adjustments. The three of us have shaken down quite comfortably, give or take a few hiccups! It's not always sweetness and light, but we have our strategies for dealing with the tougher times, and thoroughly enjoy the good times.

What we hope to do in this short book is to give interested people an insight into the processes and necessary procedures and some of the difficulties and practical details with which we have had to grapple, not forgetting to describe some of the ways in which we have all gained. You might like to start with a (fairly!) light-hearted questionnaire just to see if this kind of venture really is for you.

Points to ponder

There are no really right or wrong answers to these questions, just suggestions as to how people might react in certain situations. Many of them have been put to us by other people, reflecting very real worries that they felt we should be addressing. However, bear in mind that although none of us will necessarily react in the same way two days running, there is a serious point to all the questions, and we know of at least two friends who have opted out of the possibility of sharing a house because of some of the points raised. Needless to say there are many more than three responses to each question, but how you react to them should help to concentrate your minds! (We have tried it on ourselves and put our own answers in brackets underneath each question!)

Someone has eaten the last pot of yoghurt in the fridge. How do you react?
> *a) Must remember to put it on the shopping list.*
>
> *b) That's too bad! I must find out who it was. I wanted that for my supper.*
>
> *c) What else is there I can have?*
>
> (A, C, A) (She doesn't like yoghurt anyway!)

There is one particularly large and beautiful room in the house you are considering. How will you decide who has it?
> *a) I don't really mind. Maybe X should have it, her sewing takes up a lot of space.*
>
> *b) We'll have to draw lots.*
>
> *c) I really must have it – I need the light/view/space.*
>
> (A, A, A)

You like to entertain the family to meals quite often. How would you deal with it?
> *a) I think the others should go out and leave me the kitchen and dining room.*
>
> *b) We'll have to be flexible and 'book' the time in advance.*
>
> *c) I'd assume we'd all be sensitive to each other's needs and play it by ear.*
>
> (C, B, B)

How would you deal with housework?
> *a) We'd have a fairly strict rota of responsibilities, lists to tick things off.*
>
> *b) I expect it would all get done somehow.*
>
> *c) We could look at the cost of a cleaner for shared areas.*

(C, C, C) (For preference, we'd all do without! housework that is!)

How would you decide who did the cooking?

a) Whoever feels like it! (And if nobody does we go out!)

b) Definitely a rota, everyone would have to pull their weight.

c) I'm a rotten cook, they'd hate it. Y loves it- I'm sure she'll do most of it.

(A, A, A) (It's amazing that most times somebody does feel like it)

What would you do about shopping?

a) I can't drive so I couldn't be expected to do much.

b) We'd have to have ongoing shopping lists, whoever was available would do it.

c) We'd work it out as we went along.

(B, B, C) (As a matter of interest the non-driver quite often does shop making use of taxis)

How about the housekeeping money?

a) One person would hold the purse and dole out the money as required.

b) Make a note of what you spend as you go along and divvy up once a week.

c) Everybody would need to account for everything or it might be unfair.

(B, B, B)

Who's going to pay the bills, write the letters and make the telephone calls?

>   *a) Each person will have to have an area of responsibility.*
>
>   *b) We'd need to wait and see what everyone's strengths are and agree on who does what most of the time.*
>
>   *c) It'll all work itself out – no need to worry about it – I never have!*

(B, A, A)

You can't agree about the picture to go over the fireplace. How would you resolve it?

>   *a) We could each make the choice for one particular important spot.*
>
>   *b) We could take turns to choose a picture to stay there for, say, six months.*
>
>   *c) I would insist on the picture of my choice – I have more artistic know-how.*

(A, B, B)

The stair carpet needs renewing. How would you go about choosing it?

>   *a) I would have to stick out for what I wanted – it matters too much to me.*
>
>   *b) Go together to look at colours and designs and try to reach a consensus.*
>
>   *c) I can't imagine that it would bother me that much – I'd go with the majority.*

(B, B. B)

Would everyone need their own telephone?

>   *a) Definitely! I could not share a phone line.*

b) Whatever for? I don't use the phone all that much.

c) We could try it for a few months and see how it works out.

(A, A, A) (Take any of our phones away and we'd probably have nervous breakdowns!)

What arrangements would you want to make about mealtimes?

a) We'd all cook when we felt like it, wouldn't we?

b) There would have to be set times or there would be chaos.

c) I expect we'd eat together if we all wanted to, but no obligations.

(C, C, C) (Except when feeling fragile!)

There's enough money for central heating or new carpets - which would you go for?

a) Maybe with careful budgeting we could do both – if not immediately, later.

b) Carpets – there are plenty of ways to heat a house.

c) Central heating – we must be warm and comfortable.

(C, C, C) (one remarked that she didn't fancy wrapping herself in a carpet to keep warm!)

Would you expect to do most things with the other members of the household?

a) Certainly not, I would get on with my own life.

b) I'd expect to retain my own separate life, but enjoy company when we all want it.

c) Yes, that's the point of sharing, having company and people to do things with.

(B, B, B)

Would you mind revealing your financial circumstances to others?

a) Not at all, we'd have to be up front if we are buying a house jointly.

b) Definitely, my finances are my own affair.

c) I'd reveal what was really necessary, but I wouldn't be too happy about it.

(A, A, A)

One person wants to bring a large and hideous Victorian sideboard. Where do you put it?

a) Give in and let them put it in the rather small dining room.

b) Insist that it goes to the junk yard.

c) Suggest that they put it in their own room.

(C, C, C)

One of you has a cat and the others are not too keen.

a) Surely we should sort out all that before we start? People can't be expected to give up their pets.

b) I can't abide cats. They'd have to get rid of it.

c) As long as it was kept out of my room I'd be prepared to accept it.

(A, A, C)

What if one of you becomes severely incapacitated – mentally or physically?

a) Let's worry about that if and when it happens.

b) They would have to leave as soon as possible.

c) We would need to discuss contingency plans from the beginning and have something written into our agreement.

(C, C, C)

Many of the problems raised by these questions will be dealt with in later sections but they should give you some talking points. Maybe if your group's answers vary too much you should think again!

(Phew! That's a relief! we totally agreed on over half, and on all the others at least two of us gave the same answer. This was light-hearted but we can all think of friends who would respond quite differently and with whom we probably *couldn't* share a house!)

Do You Really Want to Share a House?

We hope that by the time you have finished this book you should have some idea as to whether or not house sharing is for you. In Appendix A you will find a slightly more serious questionnaire to help you to make up your mind. Maybe it would be a good idea to fill it in before you read any further, and then look at it after you have finished the book to see if your reactions are any different.

Obviously, the first and most sensible question to ask is 'what's in it for me?' Several of our friends have fallen at this first hurdle. It is, of course, closely linked with the other question – 'what will I be giving up?' For some people the surrender of even a small part of their autonomy is simply not a possibility and the theoretical advantages are no substitute. One friend, who had expressed great interest in the idea, began to think of so many provisos that she laughed at herself. 'I must have – a separate front door; a separate dining room; guest rooms etc etc!' After which she decided to stay in the very pleasant house which already provided these requirements.

This is the point to work out your own mental balance sheet or draw up your pros and cons – whatever technique you personally use to help make decisions. We three have slightly different reasons for being here. What we all have in common is a wish for a balance of companionship and independence and the practical economies that go with a shared roof.

As to what we have given up, again this does vary. There are undoubtedly things which we all regret a little. Some friends do seem to have faded into the background, families have had to make adjustments, sometimes one more compromise can seem one too many. Complete autonomy is clearly one of the things we have all sacrificed. There is less elasticity in this kind of arrangement than there is in a marriage or family set-up. Families can kick at each other and survive; in some ways maybe they have less choice! We have to beware of kicking too hard – there are not the emotional and conventional ties that cement family life. We survive on friendship and tolerance; push either to the limit and we founder.

On the other hand there is some comfort in knowing that we are not irrevocably committed – there are escape routes, even temporary ones! We can go away for a few days without anyone reproaching us, we can retire to our room and sulk for days if we wish, secure in the knowledge that the others will just shrug their shoulders and get on with their lives. We don't have to tell anybody else where we are going or when we'll be back. In fact, these things rarely happen; we do usually have a rough idea of what each other is doing – we're female and curious and like to share a lot of our 'doings'. Nevertheless, if the chips are down we are not responsible for other people's emotional health – the support and TLC we all offer to each other from time to time are given out of friendship not deep obligation.

There are words we shall probably over-use – *tolerance* is one, *flexibility* is another! Some people would be very disturbed by the loose arrangements by which this house runs. There are no fixed meal-times – we probably do eat between 6. 30 and 7.30 pm more often than not, but it's not a rigid rule. There are no rotas, so housework is another moveable happening; someone may get up and feel the need to clean the house from top to bottom and that's fine. On the other hand, it may be hardly touched between one fortnightly visit from our cleaner and the next. Having said that, readers will be relieved to know that kitchen and bathroom really are kept spotless at all times and nobody counts how many times who does what! Breakfasts are moveable feasts, so are lunches. It's not unknown for one or more of us to get up and take the dog to the sea at 8 am or earlier, leaving the rest of the day for more serious pursuits. In short, we are a fairly flexible lot and we have friends who view this flibberty-gibbet attitude to life with some disapproval. These are the kinds of things that you really do need to know about each other before you move in.

This raises the question as to how well do you need to know each other before embarking on such a venture? It could be argued that younger people do it all the time; university students set up house together on very little acquaintance, as do young professionals. Television is full of sit-coms illustrating some of the pit-falls! However, in later life there are some rather important differences. First, people come to this undertaking with a lot more 'baggage'. Women who have been used to running their own homes, bringing up children and juggling careers as well, will quite likely have also acquired a lot of opinions, a fair amount of authority and clear ideas about what they want out of life. Secondly, if you haven't yet got there, retirement will be looming, and there is the prospect of a lot more time spent at home and at leisure (well, that's the theory!) Whatever happens, the house sharers are going to see rather more of each other than young people running hectic lives. Finally, there is an assumption that the venture, if not seen as total permanence, is nevertheless likely to last for a few years, not just until the end of the degree course, or something better comes along! Although, of course, we are all more than old enough to know that situations can change very suddenly and drastically!

It would, therefore, seem sensible to get to know possible sharers reasonably well. So how do you find others likely to be interested? This is not an easy one. The first two of us were fortunate, in the beginning, to have met through our local U3A and discovered some mutual interests. For those unfamiliar with the idea of the University of the Third Age (U3A) - to give it its posh title – it is an organisation for older people no longer in full-time paid employment or raising families, providing opportunities for educational and social activities run by the members themselves. These can range from anthropology to zoology, taking in bird-watching, history, philosophy, walking, and line-dancing, etc etc, on the way! – whatever strengths each particular group has to offer. As we've already mentioned, general interest in the idea evaporated quite quickly, but probably floating the idea in a sympathetic group is one way of discovering if there is anybody out there on the same wave-length. The two of us who had already taken the plunge and shared the first house were then very fortunate to find more interested people through an Older Women's Network; this time we were able to talk from our own experience and several women were definitely interested, although not necessarily able to follow through at that time. Luckily, there were two of them who were willing to try and we were able to set phase two in motion and start looking for a larger house.

Maybe suggesting a discussion on the subject to any group containing a number of older women is one way ahead.

Some people have actually tried advertising in the local press, and one larger group in the south, some of whom met in this way, got together regularly for quite a while in order to get to know each other better and plan together for their venture. We shall discuss other scenarios for house sharing in a later section and clearly every group, however large or small, will have its own agenda.

Careful planning is vital to future success. We discussed everything endlessly in the beginning, and still missed important factors. How much worse off would we have been if we hadn't got at least some of it sorted out before hand! Never underestimate possible difficulties; this is one situation in which glossing over areas of possible tension is definitely not an option. To set off with fundamental differences in lifestyle, basic philosophy, attitudes towards house keeping etc, is not a good idea, however much you may like each other. We all have very dear, long-standing friends with whom we know it would be quite impossible to live. If religion or politics are of desperate importance to you don't try sharing with someone who holds diametrically opposite views. This is not to say that you have to agree about everything – heaven forbid! – but if someone has strongly held opinions which are going to be challenged daily, life could become rather fraught. Good natured argument is one thing; constant bickering is another.Finally, only you can make up your mind whether or not you really do want to share a house. We intend to illustrate what we perceive to be some of the advantages but we hope to be equally honest about the down side. Nobody can foresee exactly what areas are going to be of individual concern. Something that is quite acceptable in a family or normal social situation may drive someone crazy in a shared house. For example, we have an elderly friend who has a highly eccentric method of washing up – all her friends simply laugh

or shrug their shoulders and leave her to get on with it. On a daily basis I doubt if any of us could refrain from murdering her after a week! One's own children leaving everything lying around the floor is one thing, putting up with it from a house 'mate' is another. (It's all right! None of us actually does that!)

Remember, if you do decide to go ahead, it's going to be a lot of effort setting it all up and even more of an effort to take it all to pieces again! It's worth spending a lot of time thinking and planning.

Do you really want to share a house?

A QUESTION OF SPACE

~ OR HOW TO CHOOSE A HOUSE!

If you asked any of us what problem or problems have given us the most difficulty we would almost certainly respond with Space! This is not necessarily a matter of dimensions of rooms but involves much more subtle points for consideration. When the original pair set about planning a shared roof we spent a lot of time deciding what kind of house we wanted/needed. We had a points system to enable us to rate every house we looked at in terms of overall suitability. This system reflected our particular needs at that time, and, in the light of experience, would probably be different now.

One of the commonest questions we have been asked is- how did you manage to agree on a house? We shall look at this in more detail in the Section – *Buying the House,* but we were fortunate the first time round in that we both wanted to move, one from a rural retreat which had proved less desirable than she had hoped, and the other from a house that had never been seen as more than temporary. We both wanted to live within reasonable distance of the town centre, and the non-driver needed to be within easy access of public transport. We both liked the stone terraced houses although we knew that this would almost certainly mean little or no garden. We knew, too, what we didn't want – anything on an estate and definitely no bungalows. Having narrowed it down to preferred areas and minimum agreed size we proceeded to look at dozens of houses. We came close to exchanging contracts on one but the vendors' vagueness over possession dates proved insurmountable – one of us had already sold and was being hounded for completion! We'll look at the problems inherent in synchronising more than one sale in a later section.

It is always dangerous to go house-hunting to a deadline, which is probably why we fell into the trap of buying a beautiful house because it was there, and not because it fitted our requirements. It was a four-storied Georgian house right in the middle of town, and it had the right basic accommodation – two receptions, three bedrooms, large cellar, bathroom plus separate loo and shower downstairs, and a small secluded patio garden. (See plan – *Appendix C*)

Two bedrooms were huge and the third was quite large in modern terms, but the reception rooms were small and the dining room was virtually a corridor with four doors off it. The arrangement of loo and shower beyond the small galley kitchen was ingenious but not very convenient. For either of us to entertain separately in this situation was quite difficult. Visitors were not comfortable having to go right up to the top floor, and if someone was at work in the dining room/study there was no way to avoid a fairly continuous stream of comings and goings. To monopolise the small sitting room for any length of time seemed churlish. We made very good use of the dry and spacious basement by converting it into a studio for the resident wood-carver plus a book store, but the stairs down also opened out of the dining room so it didn't prove to be quite the refuge we had envisaged. When two other friends, with whom we had worked in setting up an Older Women's Network, expressed a serious interest in house sharing we jumped at the chance to find a larger and more suitable house. We felt that this time we could draw on our experience with the first one to get it right. Finding it was, in many ways, a matter of luck plus the ability to make split second decisions! Thanks to an alert estate agent we found what we wanted, a large house in fairly good condition, a mile from town.

We shall look at some of the problems in the actual buying process later, but having been fortunate enough to find a house that we all four liked, and which seemed to fulfil our criteria, we were then faced with the allocation of space. This had been fairly straightforward for two but how were four going to manage? In fact, we managed very amiably! This was, of course, a much bigger house – four storeys, with three reception rooms, five bedrooms, bathroom and separate loo, plus large and somewhat damp cellar.

So how did we go about allocating space? It seems obvious that everyone would want their own bed sitting room but the overall layout of any house is going to dictate the location of rooms, both private and shared. How do you decide who has what? This wasn't really a problem for us, we were all quite happy with the final allocation but there were friends who made it very clear that they felt some of the choices were 'unfair'.

Why has she got a bigger room than you? Poor you, fancy having to make do with the attic room! (The occupant asked specially for it!) Aren't you a long way from the bathroom? Isn't your room rather dark/ draughty/cold/ without a nice view?

In fact we only looked at houses that either already had more than one loo/bathroom or shower or could be easily adapted, checked that no-one had violent objections to anything on offer, and discussed fully what alterations were needed before we even thought of signing on the dotted line. One of us does now have a much larger room but it also serves as her studio which takes the pressure off finding space for wood-carving elsewhere. One of us spends a lot of time hunched over the computer in the study which she also uses for tutoring, but nobody minds; it doesn't exclude others from using the room – or the computer! The key to all this tolerance is, and always has been, negotiation, but it has to be admitted – it is the relatively easy bit!

Much more challenging is learning to negotiate the use of common space. We are actually living more communally than would suit some people, bearing in mind that separate cooking and bathroom facilities would mean finding a larger and correspondingly more expensive house. For us this was not an option, we bought at the limit of our budget. Contrary to most people's preconceptions we have not found sharing a kitchen any great problem, but we have enough friends expressing amazement at this to realise that it could well be! We survive because we are all virtually vegetarian (a little fish creeps in here and there!) and luckily share very similar tastes in food. Having a carnivorous lodger for a while in our first house showed up some of the potential problems of mixed cuisines all too clearly – not least the smells! More importantly we are none of us 'jealous' cooks – we do not see ourselves as having greater skills than each other and if someone else wants to cook that's fine. Mostly we do eat together but there's no obligation.

We have two televisions and two video recorders – so far we have all resisted having them in our private rooms – but we still tend to finish up watching together. Nevertheless, we are all very aware of the need for choice. We are lucky in that we have two sitting rooms and a study which means that we can actually occupy separate rooms if we wish. Plenty of basement storage space doubles as a laundry room which solves the problem of what to do with other people's washing. This had come close to giving us a real headache. The two who saw the patio as a place to sit about in the sun with wine bottle and glasses were somewhat at odds with the one who had dreams of washing billowing on the line. However, a carousel line in a discreet spot in the garden plus the laundry room have provided a compromise reasonably acceptable to everyone.

Gardens can be another source of friction. Two of us have always gardened fairly seriously – well, one of us very seriously – major therapy stuff! This in itself could have caused difficulties. Finding the kind of property we wanted with a sizeable garden would have cost a lot more than we could afford, so both houses have had smallish patio/backyard gardens – this one does have a reasonable front garden as well. The third member is into vegetables, but there was distinct resistance in some quarters to growing beans up the front windows. Solution? An allotment. It seemed like a good idea even though one of us is congenitally idle when it comes to physical work, one has a bad back and the third whilst appearing to have boundless energy has a tendency for it to trickle out through her toes from time to time, with spectacular results. Sadly, the idea has died the death due to a bad summer, unexpected back problems for the two who'd boasted of their potential muscle power and not as much other help available as we'd hoped. It could have been another space to escape to, but no hard feelings that it didn't work. You have to be prepared to experiment and sometimes fail.

The word escape is quite important in this context. Acceptable space is not necessarily about dimensions. It is far more about the business of sharing with other people, whether within a family set-up or in a shared situation of any kind. For some people having a separate front door is vital; for others it might be a garden, a work room or a study. People vary enormously in their ways of creating their own space. For one person escaping into their head might be simple; for another actually closing a door and being right away from others might be essential. We three are all different and have had to discover each others' needs and strategies. We have also had to come to terms with the needs of other people – friends and family.

This is definitely an area in which we found our experiences in the first house very valuable. There the spaces had not worked out well for anyone. What is often difficult for everyone concerned is that assumptions about total accessibility have to be relinquished, and to some extent redefined and re-negotiated. If it's difficult for a friend or member of the family, perhaps in distress, to have instant private access to you without having to be polite to others, then you've got it wrong. Equally, people dropping in have to take into account that the members of the house may be doing something jointly.

Quite often it works out that whoever else is around has a cup of tea or coffee and then tactfully disappears. If that's not convenient then the hostess has choices – her own bed sitting room (not always a comfortable option) or two sitting rooms plus study. Having three such spaces means that in this house we could, theoretically, all entertain separately and simultaneously.

In practice, we do quite a lot of joint entertaining. For our first Christmas 80+ people flowed round the house quite comfortably – it was a very pleasant mingling of three people's friends and families. Several birthday buffets for friends and family have happened here, simply because we have the space to do it. Of course, this is always after consultation with the other two – nobody's objected so far. Indeed, it's gone a long way towards breaking down barriers and giving us all a sense of extended family. However, the important thing is that we do all retain our separate lives and identities. Families in particular need to know that mother is available as and when needed, whilst secure in the knowledge that they don't have to worry about her being alone. Granny in the chimney corner seems unlikely to be our fate!

However, anyone embarking on this kind of venture may find that some friends tend to disappear. Some actually took us aside and issued solemn warnings, one dismissed us in exasperation as 'one nutter having found another.' It can be quite difficult to hold steady under a barrage of criticism and disapproval; this can shake one's confidence in the rightness of what one is doing. Some friends opted out and have not returned, and this too has been hard. On the other hand, there are those who may have gulped a little in the beginning, kept their private reservations to themselves, and hung in there providing the shoulder to cry on, the tea and the sherry, and generally being good friends to all of us.

One very old friend made the journey from the south, with her nephews in tow, to make sure that all was well. It was quite hilarious being vetted by two solemn young men. Fortunately they seemed satisfied with what they found and relieved that life-long honorary aunt hadn't done anything too silly.

Basically, two years into the second experiment we are reasonably pleased with the way we have managed to 'use' the house to our joint advantage. There are still areas to work out; the upstairs sitting room is now finally finished but still tends to be used as an extra guest room but not much else. We have run out of both money and enthusiasm to expend on outstanding decorating and a few minor repairs and improvements. The allotment absorbed a lot of energy and the garden continues to do so, although it is beginning to flourish. But above all, we have kept talking; there are constant small changes in any household, and when you are accommodating three lots of family and friends nothing stays still. What works today may not work in three months' time – we may yet rearrange all those spaces.

And indeed we have!

> *Since writing this section, we have had some major rethinks, not without a certain amount of trauma, but now amiably resolved. We explore these very recent changes in a later section –* Transition *–making changes? However, this in no way negates the thinking in the foregoing – it merely serves to underline the need for flexibility and the possibility of things evolving in different ways.*

BUYING THE HOUSE

Getting this right is so important that we have really highlighted the points we feel are vital. Uncertainty about any of them probably means you're not ready to go ahead!

Points to consider –

What can you afford?
Are you buying the house in equal shares?
Do you need a mortgage?
What are the likely outgoings?
Can you all afford them easily?
What criteria will you use in choosing a house?
What legal points need to be considered?

Finding a house to suit oneself alone can be difficult. Believe us, finding one to suit two or more people with probably very different needs and life experiences is even worse. Clearly, agreeing a price range has to be the first hurdle. Ideally, it is best to own the house in equal shares, but if circumstances dictate otherwise it shouldn't be too much of a problem, provided legal advice has been given, and taken! In deciding how much each can put in, the same rules apply as when buying a house anyway. **Underestimate what you can afford and overestimate how much moving and sorting out a new house is going to cost!**

If possible, find a good estate agent who understands what it is you really want, and who isn't going to send you details of 2 bed-roomed bungalows in the middle of nowhere when you want a 4 bed-roomed house in the centre of town. Having found the house of your (compromised) dreams do you need a mortgage? A lot of people thought that we would find this an insurmountable difficulty – two unrelated females of mature years in the first   instance, and then, later, four of us? Impossible they said. Not at all, said the Building Societies. Apparently, they positively welcome pensioners – one section of the population that isn't going to be made redundant and has a relatively predictable income.

An important point to bear in mind is that anyone lucky enough not to need a mortgage will still have to be included on the mortgage deed. This can be a source of difficulty; our fourth member, perfectly legitimately, reminded us that if we pre-deceased her she could find herself liable for the mortgage payments during the interim period before disposing of the property. This was amicably solved by setting up an insurance policy to cover house expenses for a year, something that was provided for in the Trust Deed anyway. (We'll come to that later!) The great thing to bear in mind is that the shares in the house can be provided by each individual according to their means – all cash, part mortgage, all mortgage if the Building Society is happy with the arrangement. It could look like this –

Cost of house - £100,000
A provides £25,000 cash
B provides £10,000 cash   £15, 000 mortgage
C provides £20,000 cash   £5,000 mortgage
D provides no cash   £25,000 mortgage

A mortgage of £45,00 would almost certainly be acceptable to the Building Society and the monthly payments would, of course, be pro rata - B pays 1/3, C pays 1/9 and D pays 5/9. The Society will be totally uninterested in who pays what as long as it's paid, and that all parties have a suitable income. Be prepared for quite long interviews, at which you will all need to be present, and at which your personal finances will be laid on the table for all to see. Some people find this idea very threatening but we haven't found a way round it so it's something to consider quite carefully. It doesn't mean that you have to discuss personal finance as a general topic! On the other hand, as we have found, what we can all afford in terms of the house is something we have to be up front about.

Bearing in mind that this particular group is retired, and therefore not exactly upwardly mobile (except maybe heavenwards!) the duration and type of mortgage are of some importance. The Building Society was happy for us to have a 10 year term, and implied that this could be re-negotiated in due course - as long as we'd managed to last that long! We all agreed on an interest only mortgage on the grounds that it did keep the monthly costs down, but on the understanding that we had enough capital, either available or as part of our equity in the house itself, to pay off our share. Most of the mortgage on the first house was carried by one of us, but she had more than sufficient capital tied up in the property she had not yet sold. Clearly, it is important for all parties to trust each other not to put the arrangement at risk by being, or becoming, insolvent!

Having established that a mortgage is possible, that you have an agreed price, and that you really all want to go ahead – next find your house! When looking for our original house (for two of us) we actually instituted a points system based on our then perceived needs and preferences. We awarded points out of 100 having worked out our individual priorities.

2 separate reception rooms	15
2 loos (or at least possibility)	10
garden	10
dog walking	10
near town centre	5
space for wood carving	10
3 or 4 bedrooms	15
sunny aspect	10
good repair	15
TOTAL	**100**

As you can see, some of these points were quite specific to our needs, others are going to be of concern to most people. We had two dogs at the time, one person with no car and the other with a serious wood carving habit! We both love gardening, and sunshine is very important to us. Any group of people will surely find other points that will be vital to them personally and on which it would be dangerous to compromise. As already mentioned we did compromise on the first house in terms of common space and it created some real problems. However, the points system can help. Anything scoring less than 75 was usually discarded, which meant that we didn't tramp round too many houses that were definitely going to be no good. One house, which we both liked very much, scored well on almost everything but lacked the two separate reception rooms, and was definitely not in good repair! This meant that it lost 30 points straight away, and was reluctantly crossed off the list.

Buying for four people presented similar problems, although we were in surprising agreement as to our basic requirements. We were doing a lot of seemingly casual looking, but suddenly had our minds nicely concentrated when the bijou Georgian residence sold before it was officially on the market. It appeared to coincide with a moment when every large house in town was suddenly either sold or withdrawn from sale. One house had a lot of appeal but too high a price and an obdurate owner who, despite a not very optimistic Surveyor's report, didn't believe in negotiation. Also, words like woodworm and dry rot were being bandied about too freely, so we withdrew. There didn't seem to be a lot of options. However, this is where having the right estate agent paid off. We were gloomily surveying yet another four bed-roomed house with small rooms, little light, and a disgusting backyard, and bewailing the lack of anything remotely suitable, when Roger tentatively suggested that he knew a house that might just suit us. Would we like the details? Suffice it to say that the details were delivered to the pub where we were lunching and next morning found us viewing a very desirable property. What's more he'd just found the perfect house for the owner as well. Seven weeks later, at the end of February, we moved in!

I'd like to tell you that we all lived happily ever after – and so we did, up to a point and for some of the time! However, there were a lot of snags we hadn't expected – it was not as perfect as we thought. It very rarely is! Décor that fitted nicely with the previous owner's furniture looked quite wrong with ours. Carpets we thought we could live with had to go!

Wallpaper got summarily ripped off. Also, we all had slightly different views as to what was acceptable – all of us could tolerate different things or had violent antipathies. Sorting out priorities was our first major task, and it did cost more than we expected, in both irritation and money! But then it always does. Our contingency fund was totally depleted by the end of the summer, and we had to sit back and look at how far we'd come.

In fact, we had come a long way. We had changed most of the décor that didn't fit, we now had a minimum of three power points in each room and full central heating. The kitchen/diner had been knocked through and we had completely refurbished the top floor and put in a new loo and wash basin. There was now a separate shower room, and a basement which could double as a laundry room and general store – not to mention all the minor jobs we'd fitted in! In all this, we had been extremely fortunate in having a marvellous team of craftsmen, patient, good-tempered and endlessly inventive on our behalf. We shall always treasure the moment (round about September!) when our electrician handed back his key and remarked sadly, 'Do I have to give it back? I shall really miss coming.'

I suppose that the moral of this is that you can be sure you've thought of everything but you never have. Of course, we knew that we needed central heating and some refurbishment but we hadn't seen the whole picture because you never do when a house is inhabited by someone else. It cost us all quite a lot more than we'd budgeted for and to some extent this is holding up some of the secondary things we would like to do. Also having only three now instead of the original four has made us look very hard at our outgoings. A rather frightening gas bill has induced an economy drive in our second winter which means that we check what we are using as we go along, whilst remaining mindful of the need to keep warm. We have reduced costs, and where possible DIY is the order of the day. Fortunately, two of us are keen on painting and decorating and the third is more than happy to make the tea, so it works out quite well. Shared bills don't look so bad when you divide by three, and we keep a total of weekly expenditure so as to have some kind of average outlay. On the whole we are quite pleased with the results, but of course, larger houses can eat money, particularly when they are old as well! We are at present bravely facing the fact that our ancient water heater may be in the midst of its final death throes. Fortunately, the occasional paying guest from the University not only adds another welcome conversational dimension at breakfast but also helps to keep the boiler fund solvent!

We have already mentioned the need for a good solicitor. You may have an excellent family solicitor but he/she may not necessarily be sympathetic to the venture, or have the necessary knowledge to avoid the inherent problems. We were particularly fortunate in that one of us had a very good and innovative young man, who had dealt with a lot of shared property deals in the south. This kind of arrangement is much more common amongst younger people, but is not usually meant to be quite so permanent. He made us think round all the possible difficulties, snags, pitfalls, and then produced a few more of his own. After we had removed our heads from our hands, we tottered off to consume large quantities of coffee and wonder what we were getting ourselves into. However, we recovered our courage and put ourselves into his capable hands. The result was a Trust Deed which is elegantly simple, but very effective. We must stress that every group will need to look at its own individual needs based on the circumstances of its members. Our Trust Deed was drawn up in the light of possible complications arising from one person's particular circumstances. There are alternative ways of drawing up the legal niceties – eg Tenancies in Common – but this is where a good solicitor will act in the best interests of everyone concerned. The main points which we were advised to bear in mind are –

How might you deal with a situation in which one person needs/wants to leave?

What happens if somebody dies and the house has to be sold to pay the appropriate share to the estate of the deceased?

As already mentioned we've managed to sort out the first situation very amiably. At that time we decided against finding a replacement, although this might be a future option provided those remaining were in total agreement. If somebody dies we have written in an obligation on the part of her heirs to pay the basic house expenses for a maximum of one year, so that the survivors have time to think.

Occupation of the house must be for sole use of the parties involved.

This is important. The example given to us, by our solicitor, was that supposing one of us died and had a relative staying at the time, there might be an assumption that they could stay on and take over the share. Without a specific caveat this could cause legal problems.

What do you do if someone becomes ill – mentally or physically?

This bit of the Trust Deed is laughingly known in this house as Clause 4! invoked whenever anyone appears to be behaving irrationally! Seriously, every group will have its own answer to this problem, but it does need to be put into legal terms. None of us wishes to be a burden to the others and if serious problems arise we have allowed for action to be taken by them, in consultation with our families. Of course, we help each other through minor ills and difficulties but long-term care is not part of the deal.

What happens about the furniture etc that each brings to the house?

We have assumed that all furniture is jointly owned unless specifically indicated, preferably in writing and agreed beforehand. We all have 'bits and pieces' that families will want to hang on to. Equally, if it comes to a split up then each must have enough to set up house again, separately.

Of course, the actual Trust Deed is full of 'whereat's', 'heretofore's' and 'aforesaid's' and lots of legal nitty-gritty, and your own solicitors, knowing the individual circumstances, will advise on any specific knotty problems your particular group might encounter. Certainly, we had good cause to be grateful for such a tightly drawn document when we had to unpick part of our arrangements, not because of any ill-will but simply because there were no ambiguous areas to throw up unforeseen difficulties.

There are some diagnostic questions in *Appendix A* which should help you to work out the right answers and provide some more thinking points.

Finally, before embarking on this kind of venture there are things which everyone must consider from a very personal point of view. You may be thinking of tying up your capital in the joint house, but do you have children/grandchildren who might need your help? It will be legally impossible to raise a personal loan on your share of the house. How sympathetic are your family? If you are a close family their views will be important. It will almost certainly be necessary to alter your will to take into account the arrangements to be put into operation when one of you dies. Are your family prepared for the fact that your estate may not be fully available until a year or more after your death?

We hope that all this has not frightened you off! Read on ~ there are lots of benefits!

Making the Move

If moving one person or family is considered to be one of the most stressful experiences then prepare for a lot more stress moving two or more separate households into one house. If there are other sales to deal with then synchronising them can present nightmare scenarios. Our first move, involving the two of us, was complicated by the fact that one house sold rather quickly, whilst the other was affected by the temporary collapse of the rural market. In fact, we managed to get round this by having a larger mortgage of which the non-seller paid the lion's share. Remember, as we've already pointed out, Building Societies don't care who pays what as long as they get their money, and they are satisfied that you can all afford it. The buyer for the house that sold fast was extremely pushy, totally uncooperative and not in the least interested in our problems, but we all know that's often par for the course! The point to bear in mind is that with more than one sale involved it can all get very fraught indeed. We survived with the help of good solicitors and a very helpful estate agent, but it was not easy.

Moving into our present house with four of us was a potential nightmare but, as it happened, there was only one sale involved and it was amazingly simple. What was complicated was the actual legal process. There was a point when we all sat round the table whilst our solicitor sent the forms to sign in one direction, and we passed the sherry bottle round the opposite way taking it in turns to sit with our heads in our hands. Fortunately, our original Building Society was willing to give us the necessary mortgage although not without another lengthy question and answer session. This was quite traumatic, particularly for one member who was less than happy about discussing her finances in public.

Furthermore, this stage can be complicated by the difficulties inherent in trying to get all the necessary monies available simultaneously. With three separate business arrangements to be made it proved impossible for everyone to provide the agreed share of the cash on time. As it happened we were spared the problems of bridging loans only because one of us had sufficient capital, not to mention generosity, to keep the transaction afloat, and very grateful the rest of us were. We could have lost the purchase, not to mention finding it very difficult to keep our team of workmen paid as we went along. This kind of situation does test the degree of trust necessary to survive a potentially damaging crisis. We came through that particular one with flying colours, and it has somehow made it easier to deal with our everyday finances knowing that we can be that flexible if the need arises.

Having fixed a moving day, ordered the removal van, or vans, what next? We staggered our moving days; one lot came in on the completion date, and the others a day or so later. We had agreed on which room was which, and had some kind of plan as to where furniture was to go but things like sorting out the kitchen had to wait until we were all available to make decisions. Bearing in mind that putting together several households will involve acquiring surplus fridges, washing machines, cookers, etc, there needs to be some discussion on what to retain and what to get rid of. Because two of us had been there and done that and it had been agreed that it suited the other two to bring relatively little, this wasn't a great problem. We took over the resident cooker but the washing machine and drier, plus two fridges, a freezer and a microwave fitted into place quite easily. Because we were having a great deal of work done on the house it took several months for us to achieve a reasonable semblance of order. In some ways this was a definite disadvantage; because we muddled along for that period, inertia set in and it probably took us longer to decide on how we wanted to arrange cupboards and to organise the kitchen and dining area. This is never going to be easy with several women all having their own idiosyncratic views on what's best! There is a danger of winding up with the kind of compromise which really satisfies nobody.

The piles of boxes were with us for months and then caused us more problems when we opened them up and discovered all the things we'd forgotten we possessed! And if we hadn't used them in so long did we really need them? Other people's trappings – the kind of things you can't quite bring yourself to get rid of - can be both boring and a nuisance. The large cellar took care of all these problems for a while, it did give us some thinking time – there are still things festering down there, although it must be said that Oxfam has done rather well out of us.

Equally, the question of whose crockery, cutlery and cooking implements generally can be a mine-field. Women are amazingly partisan about things like cooking knives! For instance – 'who has removed my favourite knife which I have had for 40 years and without which I can cook NOTHING!?' Or maybe – 'How dare you put my frying pan in water – water has never touched its surface in 25 years!!' On the whole, we have managed to defuse most of these problems; we use a judicious mix of different crockery and cutlery and have got used to each other's saucepans and implements. Some things we have bought new and jointly, like an array of jolly mugs and a rather smart toaster and cafetiere. This is the fun side of sharing, and, for us, clashes over choices of this sort are relatively few.

Furnishing our own bed-sitters was easy enough; we all provided what we needed, chose and paid for our own floor covering and made our own decisions about positioning radiators and power plugs. The common rooms were very much organised by consensus; nobody has the power of veto, any two can outvote the third. This situation did not arise during the brief time there were four, but we would have had to consider how to deal with possible stale-mate and we would urge any group to decide on their strategies before-hand. It really is too late when the argument is in full flow, and the issue has to be decided one way or another.

So, if you've managed to get yourselves moved in, and you're all still speaking to each other how are you going to deal with the nitty-gritty of the daily routine? The next section may provide some of the answers.

S ETTLING IN

One of the first things you discover when the last box is finally unpacked and the last workman has presented his bill is that you will probably all have very different styles of housekeeping. You may have visited each others' houses and formed the opinion that they did things pretty well the same way that you do – ie the right way! The problem is that two, three or four different ways of being right can be rather hard to reconcile. Probably the best way to illustrate what we mean is to describe how we have organised ourselves, based on a lot of trial and error mixed with a lot of irritation, and how we have arrived at the necessary compromises.

Almost without exception the first question people ask is about finance. Strangely enough it's probably the least of our problems! As already outlined, we have a joint house bank account. Every month we each pay in the agreed sum to cover mortgage, electricity, gas, council tax and water rates, plus enough to ensure a contingency fund for repairs, decorations, etc. Any large expenses are negotiated either from the common fund if we've got enough in it, or from our personal savings. For example, we've just bought new carpet out of the contingency fund, but if we do have to have a new boiler we'll probably need to dip into our own reserves. This will require negotiation because it cannot be assumed that each of us will have sufficient money at that particular moment. On the whole, this kind of problem hasn't given us too much difficulty. Maybe if one has the money the others will pay their share later, or work out some kind of instalment plan! So far there has always been a way to solve it, given trust and goodwill all round.

Everyday household expenses don't really give us any problems either. We tried the 'common purse' system in the first house; we both put in an agreed sum each week from which we reimbursed ourselves for whatever we spent. Probably its only benefit was that we did get some idea of how much we needed to budget for; generally, it was a nuisance because we both kept forgetting to take out what we were owed or else there was nothing left to take! After less than three months we reverted to a list on which we wrote anything we spent for the house or house-keeping and made any adjustments weekly. This works equally well for the three of us, bearing in mind that the onus to collect what is due is down to each of us individually. For example, A may have spent £30, B £23 and C £19 making a total of £72, and a debt of £24 each. B, therefore, will pay A £1 and C will pay £6. In answer to the unspoken question some readers will be asking – and somebody always does! - if we don't trust each other to be honest about what we have spent we shouldn't be sharing a house! It's probably true to say that we are all prone to leaving things off the list of expenses rather than inventing them. One bonus is that if we are out together and have coffee or meals one person can pay and it goes on the list – none of the tiresome business of who owes what and to whom. There's usually a shopping list on the board and whoever finds it convenient will visit the local supermarket or pick up the odds and ends in town. We try not to make too big a deal of it. Occasionally we will shop as a trio in one of the bigger supermarkets, picking up store cupboard supplies and vital necessities like wine! Shopping is not one of our favourite occupations and can cause a certain amount of irritation, but we usually rise above it!

This, of course, raises precisely the question of food – what do we eat, who decides, who cooks it, and when? Fortunately, we are all near vegetarian; we will all eat a little fish but only when we fancy it, not always at the same time. However, being near vegetarian doesn't necessarily mean that we all have the same preferences. It's taken quite a while, and we've had to fight our way through a lot of over-politeness, in order to realise that we have been taking the easy way out and too often eating to a common denominator which doesn't entirely suit any of us. Of course there are meals we all enjoy - any one of us can produce our famous baked vegetables with goat's cheese, and most people would have no idea who'd done the cooking. We each have our specialities which the others will sometimes ask for. We can knock an impromptu meal together between us in half an hour with never a black look in sight. Sometimes, if the others are out, one of us will take over the kitchen and have a cooking binge. Sharing a kitchen *can* inhibit the occasional impulse to have a session baking cakes, bread or whatever. In some situations it might be desirable to 'book' the kitchen; this is going to depend on the people concerned. None of us is fanatical about cooking but I can imagine a dedicated cook finding it very frustrating not being able to allow her creative urges to have full sway!

Dietary requirements can cause difficulties and this is where too much politeness is definitely counter productive. One of us is now unable to eat curry, chilli or beans – note unable, *not* doesn't like! For quite a while this led to the other two refraining from cooking dishes which they enjoyed. This is a foolish situation to get into as it inevitably leads to some irritation if not downright resentment. It's now accepted that the wimpish one is quite capable of finding herself something else to eat and won't sit there grudging their every mouthful! It's also necessary to be tolerant of other people's seemingly odd eating habits. If someone has next to nothing for breakfast this is presumably the habit of a life time and not to be criticised. Similarly, if vinegar is what you want on your chips then that's fine too; so is not liking potatoes all that much or periodically putting yourself on the Hay diet. Learning each others' funny little ways is vital; for example, one of us has medium tea with a minute dash of milk and she genuinely finds it undrinkable any other way; it's now become second nature to the other two when making the tea. Then there's the matter of the butter dish – the butter must not look 'messed about'. Yet another bit of fussiness is the fact that one of us feels a great need for all the mugs on hooks in the kitchen to face the same way! These points may seem very trivial but observing them does help to keep irritation at a lower level.

So who does the cooking? As we have made clear earlier we are not into rotas, and again it comes down to mutual agreement, who feels like it or who's not busy at that moment. There may be weeks when one person doesn't cook at all, and someone else does most of it. However, the important thing is that it really does balance itself out over a longer period. (One of us even now is off duty whilst she slaves over the computer, producing this book!) Equally, we recently managed to amaze three guests who watched us dance – without any real discussion or argument - around our fairly small kitchen, one doing the bulk of the cooking and preparation, and the others dishing up and washing up as we went along, with the result that after the meal there was very little to do.

Also, we don't have to eat together. Sometimes people have different schedules, come home later, or simply don't feel hungry! There are no obligations and no need for excuses or explanations if somebody doesn't turn up for a meal. This has been another area where too much politeness has sometimes led to resentment. People have felt that they should inform others of their plans when, in fact, nobody was asking!

Breakfast is a moveable and personal matter. We all make sure that we have our own preferences in the larder and eat as we choose. Sometimes we do all end up at the table at the same time but early mornings, as in any household, can present problems. There are no easy answers to people's differing needs, and in any case they can vary from day to day. The migrainous one is usually quite amiable in the mornings but not with a pounding head. The quiet one can on occasion appear quite morose, and the lively one can be too lively on occasion. On the other hand, we are all who we are, and this is an area that really does demand tolerance and acceptance of differences, and we generally manage to be amiable over the coffee pot and start the day reasonably harmoniously!

Shopping works out reasonably well, although there are times when there are mutterings if somebody buys the wrong kind of jam or less than perfect bread. Of course, this has happened less often as we have come to know each others' preferences and to indulge their particular fancies. The right kind of sherry is very important, so is the right coloured Tahini! There will be black looks from one if boiled potatoes appear on the menu too often; soft tomatoes or too hard apples are anathema to some and a certain nose is always turned up at the sight or smell of a herbal tea bag! But these are all trivial matters and it's probably true to say that getting uptight about such things is more likely to be a sign of some other underlying irritation.

This may all sound a little negative but we have found from experience that it is the minor things that can really point up the minus factors. Differences in style matter more, one suspects, than when younger. Take candles! Well, 'take them away' for some, 'how can I dine without them?' for another. To wipe or not to wipe the dishes; to soak or not to soak – we could enumerate all kinds of examples, and everyone will find their own. However, it is possible to work through these differences, sometimes finding a compromise, or sometimes agreeing to differ. For example, whoever washes up chooses how to do it, and this is all right – no black looks, no criticism, no muttering. What does matter is agreement on matters of basic cleanliness and hygiene and that really doesn't give us any problems. That's where looking at each others' style of housekeeping before you move in can provide the important clues!

This brings us to general maintenance and cleaning of the house. Who does what and when? Again we have tried to avoid rotas. Once a fortnight we have a cleaner. Originally she cleaned all the neutral areas i.e. two sitting rooms, study, bathroom and shower, plus guest room. As we have altered our use of the house – something to be dealt with in the next section – our deployment of Brenda has changed and, in fact, is still in something of a state of flux as we see how best to use her. Of course we all take care of our own space and at one point had a system whereby we each took on overall responsibility for certain areas. In other words, there are a number of ways of dealing with this particular concern, and there is probably no one way that will be appropriate for ever. We try to be flexible in order to reflect the changing needs of the household and of individuals. If someone is busy on a particular project then, if at all possible, the other two will take over most domestic duties. It goes without saying that if one of us is ill the others do whatever is necessary.

Inevitably, people have different areas of expertise and experience. Two are much keener on decorating and DIY generally. The third has the tiresome habit of doing administrative things before anybody else has realised they need doing! However, the bills get paid and the correspondence does get sorted which is really quite useful. It's not a bad division of labour, and, if it comes to the point, all three of us can actually do any of the necessary tasks. One of the difficulties we have encountered is the varied response to what is known to one of us as 'tearing the place apart AGAIN!' Two quite enjoy chaos – the third, having long ago thankfully abdicated her decorating/DIY duties to more expert hands, preferably when she was away, finds it difficult. We have all had to learn to be tolerant of what seems, to the opposite view, to be quite unreasonable behaviour.

Laundry is very much a personal undertaking. As we have described elsewhere for a short time drying it became a fairly major issue, happily resolved by one of our famous compromises. We really don't have rotas for washing either. If someone is going away or has just come back with a huge pile the others will defer their own. Otherwise we will do a polite check with each other and, if necessary, negotiate alternative times. We have plenty of drying spaces which means that on occasion we can all be drying washing and booking the ironing board. It says a lot that we had originally thought of having two boards and irons but have simply found it unnecessary.

Two televisions in different common rooms should have given us enough choice of viewing, but somehow it hasn't quite worked out. More often than not we have finished up watching together in the main sitting room (admittedly the most comfortable room) and, rather like the cooking, probably watching at a rather low-key level in order to accommodate all tastes. We do have varying interests and enthusiasms. One of us finds the other two's obsession with Star Trek decidedly weird, and we have all probably politely watched things that we wouldn't normally consider. On the other hand, we have acquired some new tastes from each other, like Frasier! Our new arrangements should solve these problems. (See *Transition – making changes*)

The garden is also another possible source of tension. On the whole we have managed to compromise well enough for everyone to be quite happy with the outcome. Two of us are very keen gardeners and willing to do the bulk of the work, and to pay for any expensive plants ourselves. It seems unfair to expect the third one to finance our plant extravagances. This raises another potentially vexed question. How do we decide what to buy for the house and who pays for it? Our solicitor originally drew our attention to this problem, and whilst it really hasn't given us any trouble we are aware of the possible pitfalls. In our first house one of us wished to buy what we both agreed was a particularly gorgeous rug for the sitting room. At first, the other demurred on the grounds that she couldn't afford it but a mutual friend pointed out that it was churlish to deny both of us the right to enjoy it out of a mistaken sense of pride and so the one who happened to be more affluent at that moment did buy it, and we both enjoyed it! Generally, purchases are jointly agreed and we are particularly fortunate in that so far we have had no major disagreements. We have chosen two lots of curtains in five minutes flat, a settee in ten minutes, and a major carpet choice took not much longer. Admittedly there had been a lot of preliminary discussion and a certain amount of negotiation on colour, but no real dissent. There are occasional mutterings from the one who is not so keen on painting everything white but they are, on the whole, quite good natured and it doesn't all finish up white!

Of course, every group will find its own areas of difficulty, possibly quite different from ours. Tolerance and flexibility surely have to be the main requirements for survival. In the next section we will describe how flexible we have managed to be – we think!

Transition – Making Changes?

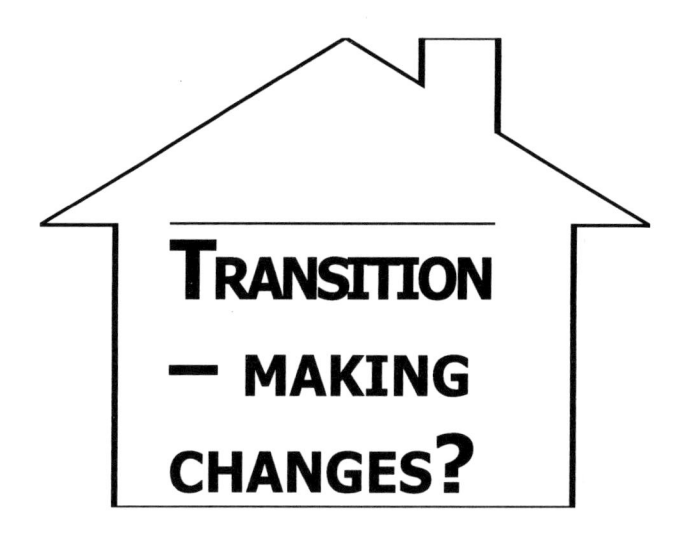

As indicated at the end of our section on Space we are, at the time of writing, just about coming to the end of our big upheaval. We have completely rethought the use of the spaces in the house (and we've moved several thousand books to prove it!) We have to be honest and say that this has not been entirely without difficulty. For the first time, there have been major disagreements which have not been that easily resolved. However, we're all still here, all still speaking, and have reached a consensus which seems to be acceptable to all of us. Each of us now has two rooms; one has a workshop and a bed-sitting room and the other two have a bedroom and study/sitting room each.

One of the problems has been that the house is bigger than we would have chosen if we had been three from the start. We had finished up with a lot of neutral space which one of us liked a lot, but she hadn't realised that the others perceived it quite differently. They were seeing these rooms as 'no-man's land' belonging to nobody but not really accessible as places to treat casually and just leave things lying around. Two of us had relatively small study bedrooms and we did tend to spill over. Also because the computer buff used the study quite a lot the others seem to have developed the habit of seeing it as off-limits. It was at this point that over-politeness (something else we go on about rather a lot!) really did get in the way. Everyone was aware of tensions but nobody seemed to be able to voice their irritations.

Communication is probably always going to be a difficulty for any group coming together in later life. Quite early on we discovered that we could all walk away from a discussion with different perceptions. One might think that a decision had been made, another would have seen it simply as an airing of possibilities and the third might have dismissed it as passing comment to be discussed later. For instance, we had talked about painting the hall and had tossed around some ideas on colour. Two of us, who had not seen a final decision as having been made, were amazed to discover that the third had actually put paint on the shopping list! Similarly, we have discovered – after five years! - a major difficulty! Ideas presented in diagrammatic form by the one who loves to produce all major thinking in this way are almost always bound to be rejected by the one who can't abide diagrams and actually feels threatened by them – she wants proper words!! This did not help our thinking processes. Keeping the communication channels open is now one of our prime priorities!

Other difficulties arose over differing perceptions of how we should make use of the house overall. One would have preferred to think about letting off part of the house to service its quite hefty mortgage. Another would have liked to consider finding a fourth member to buy in a share. The third was finding the constraints of having only one block of personal space irksome and preferred the idea of more separation. This became the preferred option – at least for two of us. This raises another point to be considered. Major disagreements when there are three of you can be very threatening for the one out on a limb. The only way forward is by persuasion, discussion and negotiation and yet more discussion and negotiation! Clearly we have succeeded in resolving the problem and have found out a lot more about each other and ourselves.

So what were the major difficulties? Well, different notions of privacy seem to have fuelled a lot of the questions at issue. Interestingly enough, it was the one who had lived alone for the longest who actually had fewer problems with the shared space. Both the other two, who had lived for longer in family situations where they had had to fight (as so many women do!) for the smallest space of their own, were a lot more ferocious in their demands for more space! It has to be said that this was the deciding factor for the third who had had unpleasant visions of living in what she felt might become a rooming house and had not understood the constraints obviously felt by the other two. Clearly if you have had to fight for every inch of space you value it more highly than someone who has always had plenty. It was persuasive enough for her to be able to reach the necessary compromise.

The dangers of the rooming house have happily receded, they were never that serious. We have agreed strategies for maximum privacy but gracious hospitality! Bedrooms remain sacrosanct but sitting or work rooms are accessible to others, if the door is open it is in order to pop a polite head round the door. If the door is shut then it is permitted to knock if it's important, but to be prepared to be rebuffed – hopefully politely! It's generally accepted that afternoon sherry may well be taken in the sunny downstairs room and sunsets will be gazed at in the top room – if invited. We are, at this very moment, planning our 'room opening' parties! and two are providing TV hospitality to the third whose room is not yet ready. However, we can now choose to view exactly what we want secure in the knowledge that, if invited to join us, our guest really does want to watch it too!

We have agreed on all the necessary work in the house to make it possible, and the house funds will reimburse all of us for expenses incurred because of the changes. It has been a great upheaval – for at least one of us, almost as bad as moving! However, we are all pleased with our new arrangements and have helped each other with decorating, moving furniture and books (oh, those books!) and choosing new colours etc. Our much decreased common area – now the kitchen/dining room – has been made more comfortable and provides more sitting for visitors as well as ourselves. We've always spent a lot of time round the kitchen table, and we still do. Having more separate space should help to reduce the chances of irritation. On days when one feels really anti-social it is theoretically possible to spend a whole day not seeing anyone! We probably all have days like that – if we are honest.

What has come out of all this is the fact that as a mutual friend put it 'We all inhabit different universes'. One person's extreme irritation can seem totally trivial to another. What is intended as helpfulness can sometimes be seen as interference; we need to be aware of our fundamental differences whilst building on our shared interests and concerns. We are, in a sense, making a new start on a lot of levels. We hope we can grow from here.

Options – Alternative Ways to Share

As a number of people have kindly pointed out to us, we have not necessarily chosen the most sensible way to share a house. Built into our situation is the knowledge that when one of us opts out, for whatever reason –feet first, deteriorating health, or simply changed circumstances – the other two will either have to buy out her share, find a replacement to buy in, or sell up. When one member opted out in the early days, for family reasons, we survived largely because we had enough money between us to buy out her share. We do know of a similar situation where as each one died the survivors moved into a smaller house, until there was only one left! It might be necessary to stagger ages in order to make that work! The larger the number the easier it probably is to deal with this dilemma. There are, of course, going to be problems inherent in any set-up. So what are some of the alternatives? Research has been done in this field and we shall deal with some of the findings and suggestions later in this section. The first part consists of mainly anecdotal material, but all the examples given are known to at least one of us.

Many older women may have looked at the possibility of sharing with established friends and we know of several such arrangements that appear to work very well. However, from our observation there can be hidden pitfalls; take the two friends happily sharing but complaining that they have no time to spare for anything because they are living each other's lives as well as their own! Then there's the woman who moved in with her widowed friend only to find herself acting as unpaid companion and general dogsbody. This makes an important point. It is probably never really a good idea to move into anybody's existing home; in our opinion, a fresh start on neutral territory is essential. At our first venture, when one house sold before completion on the new one, we did cope for nearly a month in the other's very small cottage; but the guest saw herself very firmly as just that and we survived, just about! It even worked with the dogs who both spent a month at our wonderful 'dog's hotel' and then entered the new house together very amiably.

Other less usual arrangements include a woman who lives part time with her daughter helping her with her business, whilst retaining her own house and established social round for the rest of the time. Similarly, in the very beginning we did toss around an idea, that didn't come to fruition, of one buying a house in which the other had a pied-a-terre. In theory this would have given her the best of both worlds, if she had bought a small house in Cornwall but kept a foothold in her friendship group here. A man of our acquaintance has solved the problem equally imaginatively. He lodges in a very congenial house, but spends a fair proportion of his time travelling around. Yet another acquaintance is renting a former 'granny flat' in a friend's house. At the end of this section we include a piece written by another older woman who, with her family, has put into action yet another variation.

There are numbers of communities, religious and scholastic, which provide opportunities for people to 'buy in' accommodation and join an established group of like-minded people. For one of our friends a lifelong interest in such a community allows her to live part of her time with congenial company and the rest in her own home. Religious communities may impose restrictions which need to be looked at very carefully. One friend finally opted out of buying a cottage which was part of a Buddhist community because of the undertaking never to have alcohol on the premises! These are probably not options to consider without a fair degree of commitment to the basic philosophy which underlies the particular venture.

Other shared houses have started with entirely different needs. A group of three live in three self-contained flats in a the same house with merely stairs and corridors in common. Obviously maintenance and upkeep are dealt with jointly but they have relatively little contact otherwise. Another group shares a large apartment, each with their own separate space but sharing a communal kitchen and dining area, in which they cook, eat and entertain individually. This a rather more sociable arrangement as people do often finish up eating at the same time. These are, in fact, rather younger people presumably all working, but it could suit some older women. Indeed, the key to making the right decisions in the long run is to consider as many options as possible. Some will be instantly rejected but others may repay further research.

Communes have been around for a long time, in many forms and for all age groups, and may well be what some people are looking for. However, we do know of one person who has tried living in one, and, despite spending a lot of time away, travelling, is now very anxious to leave because less congenial people have moved in. This highlights the basic problem of how far is it possible to control the make-up of the group, whether large or small? One of the difficulties encountered by those seeking to set up larger communities is that there can be restrictions that work both ways. Some will limit entry too rigorously, others will not allow for too much 'picking and choosing'; how far can vetoes be employed to bar entry to undesirable applicants? This can be a problem with housing association and local authority properties. Attempts to negotiate taking over some of their defunct buildings have foundered because there can be unacceptable restrictions on the uses of accommodation and conditions of tenancy. For example, it might not be possible to stipulate an age requirement, or to exclude men, if that is what was intended, or to refuse to accept others outside the chosen group. On the other hand, Sheltered Housing can place all sorts of restraints on selling and could possibly only work for a group who got in on the 'ground floor' and could fill the available accommodation. There would certainly be no way of controlling future intake.

Research into what is sometimes known as 'collaborative living arrangements' does show that there is a lot more going on out there than one would imagine, although not yet an enormous amount in this country, despite the fact that 43% of women over 55 in the UK live alone. Maria Brenton's research document for the Rowntree Foundation [1] has thrown up some very interesting information. She has looked at a number of communities in the Netherlands where the idea, which seems to have arisen in Denmark in the 1970's, has really taken off. She quotes American researchers, McCamant and Durrett, who describe co–housing as 'housing that combines the autonomy of private dwellings with the advantages of community living'. (p.11 – op cit) They go on to detail the common characteristics - participation by the residents in the organisation, planning and decision making process; a physical design which encourages a sense of community; plenty of common facilities; management totally in the control of the residents.

These communities can take many forms. For some, rented apartment buildings provide the necessary accommodation, but imaginative use has been made of conversions of old buildings – churches, farms, barns, etc – whilst other groups have gone for purpose-built developments. These vary in size but whilst there seems to be agreement that too small a group can lead to problems of compatibility there is less agreement as to an optimum number. The point is also made that in larger groups a wider age range is desirable. Older residents will, by definition, have less energy to fulfil the various tasks necessary for the running of the community whilst younger members can, in theory, take on more onerous duties, secure in the knowledge that they too will be able to take a back seat later on.

Betty Friedan has briefly explored some of the American models in her book The Fountain of Age[2] and Brenton (op cit) has also looked at Canadian ventures, all of which are along similar lines to the ones already outlined. However, one initiative described by Friedan is a little different. An organisation in Los Angeles called Alternative Living for Aging (sic) (ALA) was set up in 1978 ' to provide shared housing options for older people as an alternative to living alone or in an institutional setting.' (p.360) Their aim was to provide co-operative, extended family type living and they were instrumental in setting up a number of communities which appear to have been successful. A similar venture in Santa Monica provides '. . . arranged house or apartment sharing for older women or men who weren't able to continue living alone . . . but did not want to give up their independent lifestyle'.

(p.364) Some of these arrangements were not perhaps as autonomous as might be desirable; nevertheless, one of the founders of these initiatives is quoted as saying 'I believe firmly in the concept of maintaining independence through interdependence'. (p.366) This would seem unarguable and merely serves to underline the fact that there can be as many types of arrangement as there are people who wish to enter into them. The really important point is that the choices should be available, and that women are made aware of them.

Notes

(1) Maria Brenton *Choice, Autonomy & Mutual Support* J.Rowntree Foundation 1999

(2) Betty Friedan *Fountain of Age* Vintage 1994

Cynthia Thompson's Piece

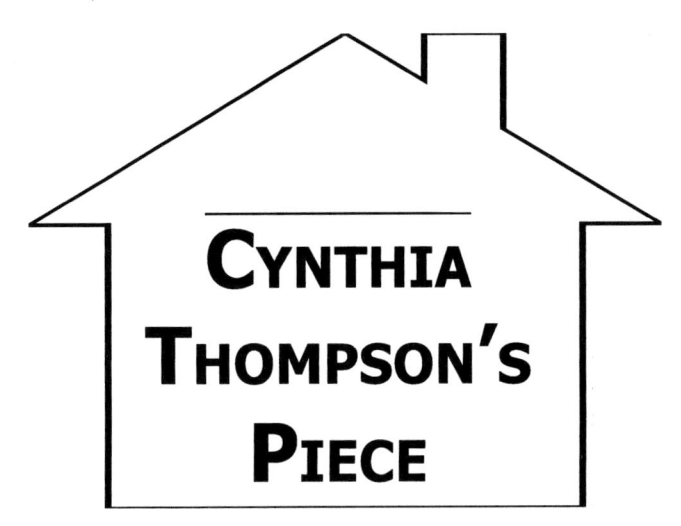

As indicated, this account has been written by a friend of a friend! Some years ago Cynthia and her husband decided to share a large house with their son and daughter-in-law. We have included it because it also emphasises the amount of thinking, planning and sheer hard work required to set up this kind of enterprise. We could certainly identify with some of their problems and difficulties.

Preamble – from a letter to our mutual friend

I gather your friends are doing something a little different from our venture: more communal and less related. I feel it has to be easier within the family, but some people seem to find their relations harder to get on with than their friends! Friends or family, the same rules apply: you have to be mutually compatible temperamentally, and very determined to make a success of living together. Also it is important for everyone to have some personal and private space, in addition to the shared rooms.

It was the cats who started it all. Caring for each others cats and pot plants at holiday times was quite a chore when our houses were more than ten miles apart, so we began to think about living nearer – perhaps next door. Then we observed that, cubic foot for cubic foot, large houses were much better value for money than small ones, and we wondered if we might risk buying a large house that could be divided in two.

First of all we went on a camping holiday together in France to see how we tolerated one another at close quarters under stress. The pattern that emerged then has persisted over the years: any friction that arose was between father and son, and was never so serious that mother and daughter-in-law could not contain and defuse it.

Once we had decided to go for it, we agreed that we needed a framework of ground rules within which to work, that would give us a clearly defined procedure for decision making and the resolution of disputes. Nothing was to be decided informally, but only by all four of us together at a series of properly constituted meetings, with scrupulously kept minutes. No action was taken that was not unanimously agreed. Of course, discussions took place and suggestions were made at other times, but all binding decisions were made and minuted at formal meetings. We had occasion, later, to be glad of these records.

Next we went house hunting – for three and a half years! We saw many houses that would have split into one substantial unit and a 'granny flat'; one that we found very attractive but which would only split horizontally; and one that three of us liked but one did not, because the aspect to the sun was wrong. At the time the three thought it unimportant, but later agreed with the dissenter and we were all glad we had stuck to the unanimity rule. Just as we were beginning to despair, and the younger generation, thoroughly tired of their small terraced house, were beginning to look at alternatives for themselves, Lynn found the perfect house for us. It was too big and grand, too expensive, had too much land, needed too much work done on it – and we all fell totally in love with it. Nothing we looked at afterwards could begin to compare.

How we managed to negotiate the purchase, and juggle the sale of our two existing properties so as to move at the same time a little over twelve months later is a long, and quite another story, the outcome of which was that Ivor and I moved in on the last day of November 1983, and Simon and Lynn joined us on the following day.

We had a rough idea of how the division of the house would be made, but could not work out the fine detail until we had moved in and could examine the house properly. We knew we had to divide the large kitchen in two, block off a passage way and put in a second staircase, but we had to live here for some months before we were able to decide exactly where and how to complete the split. Meanwhile, we had bought the house jointly as four "tenants in common" with a shared mortgage. Both couples lived in the rooms which were to be their own but shared the kitchen and the staircase for about eighteen months. We survived the kitchen–sharing without any serious difficulty, partly because Lynn enjoys cooking and I enjoy washing up, partly because in addition to the shared (very ancient) Aga we each had our own electric cooker at opposite ends of the room; and largely because we like each other and always wanted it to work out.

We had to do most of the work of division ourselves to be able to afford it. Only the new staircases (one long and two short) and new windows for the divided kitchen were done professionally. All the other brickwork, carpentry, plumbing and electric wiring were done by the two men with the wives and one of the cats as occasional labourers. (In case you are wondering, our docile and co-operative tabby towed wires under the floorboards from one opening to another quite happily.) The amount of work involved in dividing a house in terms of electrical and plumbing work is truly formidable and should not be attempted unless you have the resources to pay professionals, or very considerable DIY skills. Many times we reflected that it was fortunate that we did not fully realise beforehand what we were taking on.

Now, almost sixteen years later, we are still, all four of us, very happy with our way of life. We have been joined by two grand-daughters, now eleven and eight, and many cats have come and gone.

What are the chief benefits? For the younger generation free childcare always available for the asking, and the ability to live in a house surrounded by its own grounds with plenty of space and freedom from intrusion (except from us!) For us the security of having someone reliable and caring at hand to help us through any crisis that may occur, and the enormous privilege of sharing in the upbringing of our grandchildren, and the possibility of borrowing a car if we both want to go out in opposite directions in an evening. For us all, having someone to put out and take in the washing if it rains, someone to borrow the odd thing from when the shopping has run out, freedom from burglars (who are deterred by there almost always being a car parked outside the house); but, most of all, we enjoy one another's company. The children have a great deal more space than any of their friends, and treat our house as an extension of their own. We all go in and out of each others houses without knocking – but can lock the door if we wish.

I think the secret of our success lies in the mutual respect and affection that we feel for one another, and our determination to get on together. We respect one another's need for privacy and 'separateness', while always being there for one another's needs. Perhaps we all want our experiment in extended family living to work happily, more than we want to have our own way on any particular issue. We would not have things otherwise than they are – and the cats are well content.

Our neighbours, having read the above, agree with it all but suggested we add a caveat to anyone planning to buy a large old house, as we have done, that it is important to check its condition very carefully before taking it on. This house had been badly maintained for many years, and a great many nasty surprises held up the work of division. In the first three weeks of occupation the central heating boiler had to be replaced: then a new water main (100 yards or so) had to be laid; two septic tanks had to be emptied and rebuilt; an unsupported beam where a support wall had been taken down by some 'cowboy' had to be jacked up and fixed; various leaks in roofs needed attention; new drains had to be laid to stop a cellar flooding after heavy rain, and many other minor matters needed attention. Oh yes – and the electrical wiring was a fire hazard and had to be replaced – I could go on! Had we not had, within the family, the skills and strength to do these jobs ourselves they would certainly have bankrupted us in the first year. Now we have sailed into calmer waters, we can be glad that we had no foreknowledge to deter us from this foolhardy enterprise, which ultimately turned out so happily for us all.

> *We found this account fascinating, particularly their methods for resolving differences. Would we have found the unanimity rule easier to operate? On the whole we think not. We would probably never have got started! If two had felt very strongly about some issue and been blocked by the third we feel that it might have created resentment – we simply didn't know each other well enough to risk this kind of embargo. Negotiation is definitely our preferred method – but other groups might think differently?*

Cynthia's piece

What's in it for us?

All three of us have our own reasons for being here – we have, as they say, all come from somewhere completely different! This comes over very clearly in the following pieces and gives what we hope is a personal flavour to what has so far been an objective view of the venture.

Also included are contributions/commentaries from two other people. The first is by a mutual friend who has been around since the beginning of the venture, and the other is from Greta's youngest son who has provided an entertaining account from the younger generation's point of view. We promise that these have not been edited at all!

Last, but not least, there is a contribution from our fourth resident, about whom we have kept rather quiet!

June's thoughts
Getting the balance right

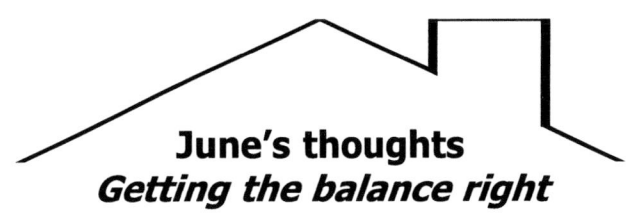

In many ways I must have looked a very unlikely candidate for house sharing in later life. I had lived alone far longer than the others, and was regarded by at least some of my friends as decidedly cranky! Certainly, I got a lot of opposition from a number of people who were clearly of the opinion that I wouldn't last six months. So why did I want to do it?

In some respects, the answer was – because it was there! Having moved myself several hundred miles north west after retirement, I had taken a big chance, but felt that, on the whole, it had come off. I'd joined various local organisations, made myself a new friendship group and settled into a pleasant enough house. However, I wasn't keen to stay there for ever – it was a bit pokey, and within three years the pleasant field that had been part of its attraction was being built on. I was already scanning the estate agents, but without much success; the slightly larger, preferably stone-built houses I coveted really were just beyond my pocket.

When a group of us started to toss around the idea of a shared roof I was definitely one of the keen ones. I saw the advantages of shared expenses and liked the idea of an altogether bigger house. Provided my own space was adequate I felt that I would not have too many hang-ups about sharing the rest of it. I also liked the idea of having people around, obviously not to live in each others' pockets, but with the choice of company available. Above all, I saw it as an interesting experiment. If all the literature about ageing is to be believed then sharing accommodation could well be a way of staying out of the nursing home for rather longer! I had always enjoyed good mutual support from friends – how nice not to have to turn out and go home after supper!

This was no where near as starry eyed as it sounds. As we've said elsewhere, we put in hours, days and weeks of discussion; we knew we had to get the right kind of house with the right kind of space. We survived getting it wrong the first time, but probably only just. Having said that, I adored the first house and resisted leaving, even though I knew that there was no alternative. Perhaps this is the first serious lesson to learn about house sharing – it only works if everyone is able to compromise. The underlying arrangements of space, routine and general ethos have to be acceptable to everyone at whatever level they can cope with. Some are less able to compromise than others; this is not necessarily a criticism, people do have different levels of tolerance. Certainly, I am about to have to compromise yet again – changes are afoot about which, in the beginning, I was less than happy but I was outvoted! So how have I dealt with this?

From the beginning, my personal strategy has been one that I have employed all my life, I keep a mental balance sheet, in fact, sometimes it does actually get written down. Of course, it can vary from day to day! If I get up feeling very crabby I may spend the day watching the scales dip ominously low. This is when I'm likely to take myself off to consider my position! Fortunately, my sense of humour usually reasserts itself fairly quickly and I'll finish the day in balance if not in credit. I suppose that basically I am aware that the balance mustn't dip too far too often, and taking on board something that is not to one's liking has to be dealt with through the balance sheet. Is there still enough in it for me? If not, what then? So far I have managed to keep myself in credit overall. Of course, the down side is going to be different for all of us. The kind of tolerance that should be inherent in family life is not so readily available among people who have come together not necessarily knowing each other very well. We must foster the necessary tolerance, but it doesn't alter the fact that other people's 'funny little ways' can come as quite a shock.

So what are the pluses? Well, obvious things like companionship come to mind, like arriving home fed up and having someone there to moan at, and to provide the cup of tea for you and make the right kind of noises. It's good to have people around for discussion and argument, and to share the joke. We really do laugh a lot. With all of us doing 'our own thing' quite a lot of the time it's always interesting to hear about what the others are doing. Then there's the benefit that quite often there's someone else who feels like a walk in the park or a photographic expedition. The down side of that is that we are all past masters at the art of persuading each other to waste time!

On a more practical level there are financial advantages. The council tax has just plopped through the letter box, and we are each paying less than half of what we would have paid on our previous smaller houses and fuel bills are definitely lower. Interestingly enough, phone bills are lower too! We can only assume that it's because we no longer need to talk to friends elsewhere for quite so long! Grocery and household bills and repairs generally don't seem quite so large when shared, although I probably drink more sherry than I used to – obviously all I needed was the excuse!

So, five years on from the start of the experiment and two years into the second house where do I find myself? Well, I'm still here and the balance sheet is still in credit. Of course I have off days, don't we all? but life presents a lot of fun and a lot of advantages. I'm willing to stick with it and see how the next phase develops.

Greta's thoughts
New beginnings

When I moved into our shared house two years ago, it was not the best thing for me to do, at the time. Not only were the four of us moving into a new house, I was also moving to a new town, my mother was moving into sheltered accommodation one mile away, and I was about to be re-located to a different town at my place of work. Instead of travelling 20 miles to work each day, I found myself travelling 80 miles along less familiar roads to a totally different location. All these events happened within three weeks. Suddenly, there was no fixed point in my life, I felt I was on shifting sands.

I mention these points because although they were all things I knew were going to happen, I completely underestimated the stressful effect. It was the little things I found most difficult, trying to memorize new post codes, phone numbers, key pad numbers, and so on. It took me some time to remember which of the eight new keys I had acquired, fitted which door. I rattled my way through each day, trying out different ones while attempting to appear competent. Any change can be stressful, even those you want to happen. We all think we can cope. All I know is I didn't cope very well. I was tired all the time and looking back I'm not sure how I managed. If you are considering sharing a house, take note of other changes which may be happening around the same time. It is very important not to underestimate the effect of too many changes at once and to build in some coping strategies before you embark on them. I wish I had!

Two years on, I have retired from full time work and found my way around my newly adopted town. I enjoy living in this shared house very much. Sharing has many advantages. The economic ones are pretty obvious, every household bill is shared three ways, household items are shared in common, economy size items and special offers can be taken advantage of, cars can be shared. The social advantages are just as important. There is always someone around to talk to, watch television with, share a meal with. 'Spur of the moment' outings which just don't happen when you live alone, suddenly become possible. We chose the house very well. Situated in a relatively small town which has a user-friendly town centre, easy to access on foot, we are also in easy reach of a number of larger towns where shops, cinemas, theatres, museums, galleries and so on are available for days out. There are regular main line train services and buses stop outside the front door. The local university also has musical and artistic events which we make good use of. We are also very near to Cumbria and north Yorkshire. All of us like to walk and get out and about, and we take advantage of the beautiful scenery almost on our doorstep. We are also very near to the sea, and have enjoyed many an evening sipping a glass of wine as the sun goes down over the bay. All of us have friends and families dropping in, which means there are often other people around and things happening in the house, which is great. Of course we have to be careful not to live in each others' pockets all the time, and to give each other space, but then, isn't this important in any kind of relationship? Having my own space has always been important to me. Sitting quietly with a good book, or listening to music is a real pleasure. Luckily the house is large enough for all of us to spend time apart, while enabling us to enjoy the benefits of being together.

Moving to a new town I knew very few people initially so it was important to me to meet people. I did this by joining the local branch of the Ramblers Association and enrolling on a few Adult Education classes. I have made many new acquaintances, some of whom I hope, will become friends. I also belong to a local photographic club which has been a real source of pleasure, enabling me to cultivate a long-standing interest in photography. One of my sons has refurbished an old bike for me to ride on. At the moment the bike is taking up space in an out-building, but I am looking forward to the spring so I can ride on the many local cycle ways we are lucky to have around the town. Quite a challenge, as the last time I rode a bike was 42 years ago!

After celebrating our two years together we are embarking on a new project. We realised that during the evenings, when not sitting around the dining table, we tended to gravitate to one room to watch television, leaving other rooms empty. We have now decided to divide up the space differently. Each of us will now have two rooms to use as we choose, which will give us more options. We all have interests that take up space so we will soon be able to spread out more. The guest room will be retained so friends can still stay with us, this is important to us all. This will leave us only the kitchen and dining room as common space. We have made the dining room more cosy by adding a small settee, and plan to add some really comfortable dining chairs in due course.

As I write this, I sit surrounded by boxes of books, videos and assorted clutter, in the upstairs room which will soon become my new sitting room. There is much to be done. It is exciting, working out where everything will fit and deciding what colour to paint the walls. Searching through some of my things, I found a card, which someone sent me, before I made the move to this house. The message inside was 'Life is full of new beginnings.' I feel very lucky to be able to look forward to a future in which new beginnings are possible.

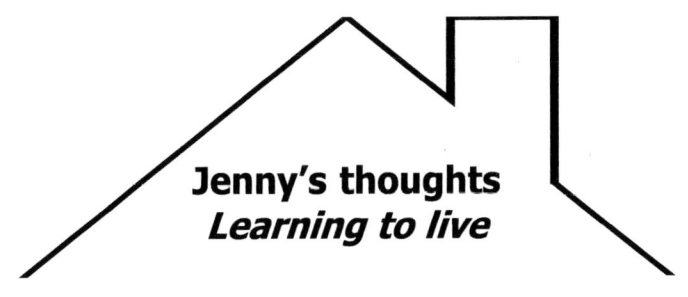

Jenny's thoughts
Learning to live

When embarking on this experimental lifestyle it is important to define clearly personal needs and aims. Each person involved must be aware of what the others want from the situation they are mutually devising. When we set about the experiment, we had long detailed preliminary discussions. We thought we had considered all eventualities. What we had not built in was a fool-proof assessment pattern for redefining our individual needs in the light of experience within the house.

We certainly were at a loss often to understand what had brought about the new need and we had to work hard to redeem lost ground. In our early days we allowed a mistaken sense of politeness to mask these misgivings, and later found it extremely difficult to discuss these glossed over areas. We have learned from this experience and now we do declare any uncertainties. Better a quick riposte now, than a developing sense of frustration and irritation. For example, I now know not to be too boisterously cheerful at breakfast time. I try not to make jokes until the morning mood of the others is clear! Other 'morning people' will surely sympathise. Another of my irritating habits, I have come to understand is that I blithely go ahead and take on a task I see as important, often without prior discussion. I live with the memory of two shocked faces regarding me up a ladder, well before breakfast, merrily painting the dining room a clear beautiful white. How could they possibly object? One did, very much. There are many other personal examples, but these two will show where my learning zone needs to be based.

We had also talked long and earnestly about personal space, and yet had not seen that a large area of neutral space does not compensate for a reduced personal one. I found this frustrating, and yet had failed to see in the example above that I had transgressed by monopolising the neutral space. I have learned a lot about myself during this venture and much of this new knowledge is not jolly.

Looking back now, I realise that often I would politely continue talking in the neutral space, when I would probably have been more content to follow my own interests elsewhere. I suspect that this applies to all of us. The remedy was in our own hands, but I know that for me a determining factor in this shared venture had been the opportunity to take part in spontaneous discussions, sadly missed when I became a widow. It seemed churlish to reject such a positive pattern when it had been regained.

Within a family one learns over the years what is acceptable behaviour. The cut and thrust of family living allows for each person's demands to be met in some measure, or possibly endured, but this is a gradual development. We had put ourselves and our idiosyncrasies into this common pot. None of us had shared any part of the earlier lives of our new companions. We took a risk. We pay the price by continually learning about one another and where the limits are for each of us. We have no experience to draw upon. The situation is new. We should have expected some difficult times.

As we grow older we think of shedding some of the baggage we have accumulated. Once loved possessions lose their charm. Some ingrown habits become unnecessary. This experiment has shown that we differ yet again, in the ways in which we approach this reduction. I am surprised and interested to find that what I can only describe as 'time to ponder' has become important. I am the gregarious, out-going one, or so I thought, and have come to see that this need for contemplation has crept up on me. What might have been a less noticeable change when living alone, is a more obvious need within our group situation. Although it is still enjoyable to eat with friends and to talk around the table I now very much relish exchanging ideas and opinions with friends tête-à-tête. There is the danger in a shared house that friends become 'pooled' and this could place restrictions on simple one-to-one meetings. Family members especially can find a shared house difficult in this respect.

The advantages are very much what I had expected when the venture began. It is good to come home to a lived-in house after time away, and to know that, when detained overnight or longer, the milk bottles will not be accumulating, that the house is less likely to have been burgled, and the great plus for me that my aged labrador will have been cared for. We have already, 'in house' jokes and we each have amiable side-ways grins at the idiosyncrasies of the others. The small rituals which cement any group we have too. Sherry is for two only, while the other 'pure' one quaffs the unadulterated fruit juice. The 'real tea' addict cannot understand how anyone can actually claim to like those smelly herb packets. Good food and good wine we all enjoy and like to share some meals with mutual friends. These are good times and we laugh a lot.

After years of shared living how do I feel? We are still here and are able to discuss the experiment; for such it is. With hindsight I would have heeded advice to keep more separate. We would then have avoided falling into the trap of sometimes sharing too many activities, thus reducing the impact of individual contributions to general conversation. By increasing our personal space within the house, as we plan to do, I think that we shall more easily come to the necessary areas of negotiation with fewer restrictions. This, I believe, will bring more contentment to us all.

We all accept that there are times when we regret not being in control to the degree that we were before we moved in together and we may decide that finally we shall live like that again. We are very different in character and we have each observed the spectacularly different ways in which we deal with the events and problems of daily life. For example, occasional bouts of ill health are met quite differently by each of us. Would we want to continue to share a house into later frailty? I think possibly not. I would like to decline privately, although it has been pleasant to be nurtured through those occasional spells of ill health in the present situation.

I see the way forward as moving towards more separateness within the shared house, retaining the tried and tested good parts, and developing new patterns based on more personal space. There is no trial run for accommodating to getting older, and I see no need for us to feel apologetic about a re-think at this stage. What would be a mistake I believe would be for us to continue a pattern which could be better simply because we are too reticent to try for improvement.

A short tale from our fourth and oldest inhabitant

I think they've kept rather quiet about me, but now I'm expected to write a short piece even though they know how difficult it is for me to hold a pen. I know I don't contribute much around the house but I do my best to be cheerful despite failing health and I suppose they do all look after me quite well – most of the time. Occasionally they leave me alone for rather a long time although they know how much I dislike it.

I have quite severe dietary problems now and they try to restrict my diet but I get round this sometimes. Not long ago we went visiting, something I really do enjoy – and I managed to get through quite a lot of birthday cake! Our hostess was most kind but they were a bit tight-lipped about it. I often think that they are trying to cut out all my treats. They mutter about 'delicate digestive systems', and I have to admit that I am on a lot of medication. Luckily I am very fortunate in the medical treatment I get from such charming people, even if they do collude in cutting down all those sweet things I love.

I don't go far these days, except in the car. Arthritis really does restrict me. I certainly can't get up and down hills like I used to, and long walks in the Lakes are not for me any more. There are other little problems. I don't always get through the night now without needing the facilities and I have to have a little help. I suppose they're quite good about that on the whole.

I have to admit that my memory isn't what it used to be. I still love to go to the sea, and thoroughly enjoy a paddle, but quite recently, after a lovely walk on the shore, I was embarrassed to realise that I wasn't entirely sure where I was! Quite disconcerting! However, they were very kind about it and took me back to the car. I also wander up to see a young cousin now and again, and have to be fetched home – most annoying.

One thing I find difficult is this insistence on privacy. I like to be able to wander about the house as the spirit moves me, and they will keep shutting doors. They don't seem to understand that I do like company most of the time. I have always found visitors a particular delight, and even more now that I'm so dependent on being taken almost everywhere of any interest in the car. I very much enjoy visiting country pubs – it's good to sit in the sun and observe all kinds of interesting people – most of them are so kind to an old lady! Crossing roads is quite difficult now; I'm a little deaf and my eyesight is not what it used to be. I may well be developing a cataract.

From time to time I go to stay at an excellent hotel in the country where I am thoroughly indulged and enjoy the company of like-minded friends. I sometimes think the people there understand me better than they do at home. I have a suspicion that this might be seen as respite care – or care in the community? I hear them talking about this Clause 4 and how you get dealt with if it gets too difficult to look after you; it's all rather worrying at my age.

My final word? It can only be - *WOOF!*

Shirley's Piece

Every time we work out the answer's to life's questions all the questions change . . .

What are my opinions on the success or otherwise of this experiment in living together?

Before I go into this in detail I should explain that I have known Jenny for over twenty five years since we taught at the same comprehensive school. June I came to know when Jenny first shared a house with her five years ago, and two years ago I met Greta when all three moved into their present house. I regard them all as personal friends now, which certainly adds a certain frisson to this writing since not all that has happened has been easy for any of them and I should be sorry if any observations fractured these friendships.

I have thought about where to begin and the viewpoint to adopt for a considerable time – should it be from a sociological or economic, a feminist, sexist or ageist standpoint? Ultimately I decided to stay simply within those areas which seem to me to be the most important in beginning to balance the equation of living together, successfully or otherwise: those of personality, finance and space.

The interplay of personalities in any group is always important and here there are three highly educated people with quite different experiences of life and equally different approaches to that life. To take the topic of change as an example: this has been very much to the fore since various changes, particularly in the realm of personal space, have taken place within this first two years of living together.

Jenny thrives on change and can cope with upheaval because she can see beyond the ensuing chaos to the end result. If she feels that something is wrong or can be improved she wants to alter it immediately and with brio, and has done so many times, especially when she lived alone. Effecting change when negotiating with others has been more testing for her. My impression is that June dislikes change, and needs time to consider what she is going to do because she finds upheavals exhausting for the spirit to cope with. I know Greta less well but, though at times she may appear somewhat firm in her views, she is outwardly calm and collected, adapting to a new situation at least on the surface, though she does not necessarily seek to alter things in the first place.

Personal space and attitudes to space have proved to be important factors as in all shared homes whether with family or friends, and of whatever size. June had lived on her own for years and was used to a house full of her own personal space; Greta had had a family around with the limitations which that imposes and Jenny had gone from a family to living on her own but finding a need to have some areas of her space filled at some time with other people: three different outlooks at base, with a need for the best compromise for each.

Next financial considerations. These have at times provided real obstacles because originally the plan was for four people to share the house and contribute to its improvement and its running; with three it can be frustrating because, with lower resources, repairs, re-decorations and renovations cannot be carried out as soon as anyone would like and some major projects have had to be put on hold. Nonetheless, it seems to me that they have achieved a tremendous amount in the two years that they have lived in the house, and despite personal variations in available capital and different outlooks on priorities at times, they have mostly established an equilibrium.

However, different outlooks, different points-of-view, different priorities, misunderstandings because of these – the seeds of conflict are here as within any group of people trying to achieve a common end, wherever it may be. 'Compromise' is that dread word which can mean that no-one is satisfied in the end and that often someone, hopefully not always the same one, is bound to stomp away, muttering, after any controversy or change.

Is it working then, given these different personalities and priorities? Are there advantages over other ways of living?

The arrangement has lasted for over two years now – not long really, in effect its apprentice period with three people, the time of learning when mistakes are made and rectified. The use of space within the house has changed radically, there are three people, not four. The question arises, but cannot be addressed here, of whether it would be a better arrangement with four or possibly five people involved.

To the outsider like myself there seem to be many advantages in the present situation, especially the companionship of people with lively and caring minds, not only every day but also when someone is, for example, ill or fed-up. There is the ability to bring another point-of-view to an individual's own problem. There are shared activities, possibly holidays together, as well as individual ones. Apart from the social side there is also the fact that each one has more space now to revolve in, in total, than if each lived alone, and yet each has a certain autonomy of their own, being able to be by themselves if they wish as well as having others there. It is also a sharing based on friendship and therefore different in essence from three people simply lodging in the same house, more akin to an adult family choosing to live together than strangers throwing their lot in.

The drawbacks? In my view it is impossible for any group of people to live together for any length of time in total harmony, and irritation of some sort is unavoidable at times. The government of the group is therefore important and interesting to observe, for with three people there is at times a danger of one, not always the same one, being polarised or edged out by the others, or possibly of families or friends adding their say or support to create a majority or to add extra tension. Sometimes an Ombudsman has seemed necessary or maybe a Solomon when storms have arisen!

A household of any sort is a living organism and, like all organisms, develops and changes. Because it is a human organism it may also be unpredictable in its development. There are, however, basic needs: it needs an environment which stimulates, it needs time, patience and a sense of humour. It needs agreed approaches in key areas such as finance and improvements.

There may be a number of reactions to the ways this household continues to develop - dismay, disbelief, hilarity plus admiration and hope of success. In creating a group with a new solution to the approach of ageing and by deciding to live together rather than in isolation - the lot of so many - they seem to have had the imagination and perseverance to make it effective.

I, for one, hope it will continue to be and to develop positively, and that I may continue to be an interested and concerned observer.

THE YOUNGER GENERATION'S POINT OF VIEW
– Ian's thoughts

Although slightly taken aback when told about her plan to buy and share a house with three other people I can't say I was totally surprised as, for my mother, it seemed like the inevitable compromise between a growing need for independence, coupled with an understandable reluctance to spend her retirement living on her own. Although the desire to move away from a more traditional domestic arrangement was strong, it seemed as though it would always be frustrated by what seemed to be too much of a leap into the unknown – personally, socially and financially. It seemed therefore an inspired decision to join with others in order to buy a house that, although being beyond the reach of their individual assets, could be comfortably afforded by a combined contribution. This enabled the purchase of a place large enough to allow personal freedom and privacy, whilst providing the security of always having other people to spend time with.

I had already met Jenny and June two years previously on a Christmas Day walk in the Lake District and was impressed by their general enthusiasm and vitality. They seemed to subvert the received notion that people of a 'certain age' like nothing better than to buy small dogs with tartan jackets, settle into a routine of twice monthly perm and set, and while away the hours knitting and purling to the beat of a carriage clock that simultaneously counts the hours to the next visit from sticky grandchildren who, with insatiable appetites, sit sullenly in the corner munching a pile of cakes and biscuits, lovingly made in preparation for their arrival.

In marked contrast, Jenny and June lived with a large, unjacketed yellow dog (which seemed to consume most of the cakes and biscuits before anyone else got a look in), had swapped the knitting needles for, in Jenny's case, a hammer and chisel with which she would attack great lumps of wood in order to produce accomplished carvings, and in June's, a word-processor which facilitated the undertaking of some rather daunting and esoteric post-graduate research. It seemed that they had fully realised the opportunities that the leisure time afforded after retirement had to offer, and had seized upon them with great gusto; not merely following the rather patronising edict that pensioners should 'keep busy', but rather pursuing interests which were worthwhile, challenging and fulfilling. Therefore, I entirely approved and agreed with my mum's choice of housemates.

Initially, there were understandable jitters about incompatibility, for they were all quite different people and it was inevitable that some compromises would have to be made. Perhaps the realisation of this led to them each being over accommodating in the early stages, as it would perhaps have seemed logical that if people share the same house they must necessarily share the same interests and spend lots of time with each other; akin, perhaps, to the spurious notion that 'a family that prays together, stays together'! Having spent many years sharing a house with others, I realised some time ago that this idea was neither practical nor desirable. It simply leads to too many compromises, causing even more arguments and fuelling resentment, until it feels as though living alone may not be such a bad idea after all!

Jenny, June and my mother seem to have quickly realised this also, and they now seem to find it unnecessary to go around in gang formation, preferring instead to do their own thing. This is not to say that they live totally separate lives, but rather that they will do things together only if and when it suits them all, and in fact this often seems to be the case.

The benefits of this are clear to see, as it has enabled three people from entirely different walks of life to come together into the same house. There was some initial disgruntled harumphing and stamping of feet over what seemed to an outsider entirely bizarre reasons; major structural rearrangements and interior décor seemed to be agreed upon almost instantly for example, but the decision over which type of washing line almost led to United Nations' involvement. However, each did manage to find their own space and maintain their desired independence.

At the same time, each found that they were suddenly the beneficiaries of the accumulated knowledge, experience and possessions of three lifetimes. Different perspectives were brought to bear on previously unexplored issues and ideas; three libraries were accumulated covering an incredibly diverse range of subjects; three lots of culinary kills were fused, adapted and improved; three groups of friends and relatives were introduced and became regular and welcome guests; cars, videos, music systems, computers, pots, pans, crockery, Hoovers, paintings, settees, tables, chairs, fondue sets, cuddly toys and countless other things were made available to whoever wanted to use them. In short, the benefits of living together seem the same as those that prompted the idea of moving in together in the first place, namely the advantages of the pooling of their many and diverse resources.

When friends at home, work or university find out about my mum's living arrangements they are often surprised and even impressed, despite the fact that they too share their accommodation with other people who were often strangers prior to their moving in. What seems to them like a logical, and in London, virtually obligatory way of living seems somehow odd in someone of my mother's age. Personally, I see little difference between them. Of course, in a rented house you have to put up with seventies décor and dodgy showers, but the reason you do this is because it makes perfect financial sense and gives you a guaranteed social life in a city that can easily leave people feeling very isolated.

It seems that for many people retirement can have a similar isolating effect –even when not living alone – and too many people seem to accept this as inevitable and inescapable. The screaming logic of the step that Jenny, June and my mother have taken seems to elude a society where exclusive ownership seems one of the unarguable pinnacles of success, whatever its cost may be. Many people would not even entertain the prospect of sharing their house with others, and often this may be the right decision; there are, of course, millions of people who are entirely content with their situation. But for those who are not, it seems that their reluctance, or lack of knowledge of an alternative, may mean that they could be really missing out on what could be the most rewarding time of their lives.

There is, of course, no such thing as a perfect arrangement – life is never that boring – but achieving a balance between communal living and independence seems to come as close as it gets. Jenny knocks lumps out of wood upstairs, June teaches anything to anyone downstairs, Mum goes on archaeological digs on remote Scottish islands, but all three seem to spend most evenings together, entertaining friends or each other, while knocking back copious amounts of sherry! Meanwhile, the big yellow dog seems to spend most of the time mooching about the kitchen, sniffing for biscuits and cursing the invention of Tupperware.

RETIREMENT? PERSONAL REFLECTIONS

Assuming that it will be in retirement or when it is fairly imminent that most women are going to be looking at house-sharing, we thought that it might be helpful to set out a few of our individual thoughts about retirement in general, how we are tackling it and how shared living has influenced what we do.

Jenny has been at least semi-retired for seventeen years (now fully – but she did escape very early!) June –sort of – for ten, and Greta for less than a year. We are all in Lancaster from choice, having moved here from other places. All of us have family reasonably close at hand; amongst us we have seven children! Two of us taught, Greta was in the Health sector. Whilst we have plenty of common interests we also have different approaches to retirement. As you will see, Jenny has a very clear idea of where she is. June is still tutoring and running weekend courses, but finding both stimulating and enjoyable enough to go on doing them for a while longer. Greta is still in the experimental stage – lots of fascinating things to try but no need to get stuck in ruts yet!

Pre-retirement courses have long recognised the need to 'learn' to be retired. It doesn't have to be about going on lots of holidays – even supposing people can afford them – it surely needs to be about finding satisfaction in living, in finally pleasing oneself, finding a pattern. It's about enjoying the rest of your life, and, hopefully, staying reasonably healthy! We've roped Greta in to make some points about health – before she forgets it all!

Explorations in Retirement
Jenny's story

In my professional life, comprising as it did firm structure, linear teaching, logical thinking, order and method and well thought-out experiments – all good left-brain stuff- I simmered and behaved myself – mostly! My colleagues would sometimes leave me speechless as they dutifully followed the pattern laid down. Amazed, I heard them extol the virtues of this imposed system. The training must have been first rate. It held. I never actually ran amok – just boiled inwardly.

I emerged from bereavement and early retirement to live alone, bemused and adrift. A chain of happy coincidences and some very good friends nudged me quietly into my present blissful area. How lucky I was to arrive at West Dean College in the early eighties to be taught by a retired master wood carver. I found good friends there and under his benevolent gaze and strict instruction came to inhabit my new world. Light years away from my early life in science, in wood I found my medium, able to explore with magic tools what each piece might offer. I have limited spatial ability and do not see a finished shape at once. I need to explore and follow the ghost shape in my mind. It has all the fun of the chase. Hours may pass with little to show, yet the mind expands and eventually the tools confidently dip into the wood.

Sculpture has always been an interest but now I look at the master works and understand genius better. The art world was not closed to me before but now I read and observe with better understanding how driven some artists are.

Would my life have been different if I had found wood sooner, or is the grass always greener on the other side? What talent I have in this area might have developed more fully and been the driving force in my life, or it might not. Who knows?

All I know is that I have found a delight in developing this ability at this late stage that charges my thinking and governs my life, and it can continue as long as I live. What fun! I feel so lucky to have arrived at this point, to live with indulgent friends in an old house with sound floors where I can work indoors or out as the climate dictates. The new house arrangements have given me a ground floor studio – Bliss! The friends are indulgent indeed. Last year as I raced to complete a commission by the due date I was excused household chores, was fed, and my moods of despair tolerated. I was even given unsolicited wine at the appropriate moments. As a retired person woodcarving I have freedom to follow my own creative impulse, and do not depend on being paid for my work. Such freedom is rarely in the gift of a younger person.

With this new life goes a totally new group of friends. I count my woodcarving teacher here as one of these friends, and we spend good times discussing wood and the work. Again I am fortunate to be a student of another benevolent man. I think that working with wood develops a generosity of spirit that inspires the teaching, and some of my happiest hours in this lovely old city have been spent working in his workshop with like-minded friends. I know that good times lie ahead and that my new studio on the ground floor will see me working with wood, listening to music and talking with friends – sometimes all of these things together!

I do understand that not everyone is able to choose totally how to spend their retirement. Often family obligations mean that time is given to caring for others; grandchildren, frail parents, or other stressed members of the extended family. Yet, at this time of retirement from paid work, if possible, it is worth looking to find what area of interest has always beckoned, but for a variety of reasons you have not been able to explore.

We talk a lot in this house about the forces which drive us now, and often around the table with friends, after starting from discussions of this house experiment, we consider other types of living in retirement. Interestingly, again and again what surfaces is the need to be positive, and to a certain extent self-centred, when taking a long look at one's retirement opportunities. Those who appear to survive best have discovered their own personal needs and have set about meeting them. No-one else has had quite your experience and so no-one can really know what those needs are. Now is the time to be quite selfish, and objectively study yourself and what course of action will give you satisfaction. As Pasteur once famously said 'Fortune favours the prepared mind'.

There is no trial run for retirement. It is here and now. Look around. Find your area, look to the opportunities and when your opportunity offers go for it!

June's thoughts on retirement

I have been in Lancaster just over 10 years, having lived for nearly 40 years in Norfolk, most of them hankering for the northern hills; I still can't quite believe I'm here. Now I only have to walk to the gate to see the Cumbrian mountains and from the little park down the road there are wonderful views of Morecambe Bay. So how did I get here?

Like many women in our age group I was well aware that retirement was not going to be financially comfortable. I had spent only half my working life in a pensionable job, and had seriously considered teaching until I was 65 in order to augment my pension. For many reasons, this turned out not to be feasible. Instead I finished up taking slightly early retirement on grounds of ill health and wondering how on earth I was going to manage. Apart from anything else what did I want to do with the rest of my life? Fortunately, I was lucky in that I did have some quite definite ideas. I wanted to have time to write, I was keen to do a degree if I could find the right course, and I yearned to move north. I'm even luckier that I really have achieved all three!

In spite of an enormous amount of opposition from family and most of my friends, moving north turned out to be a very sensible option. Property was cheaper here and I found that I could afford a modest house without totally bankrupting myself. The University offered just the kind of course I was looking for, and in theory I would have plenty of time to write. However, I became heavily involved with the local U3A at around the time I started my part-time degree and spent the next five years juggling almost as many balls in the air as I had when I was teaching. But it was fun! I had chosen to do it, and thanks to a marvellous osteopath my health had improved out of all recognition. I could enjoy gentle walks in the hills and stroll by the Bay. I could replan my garden and walk my dog. I had made plenty of new friends and my daughter had moved up to Morecambe. However, I had never seen my house as permanent (cynical laughter from friends! When had I ever seen a house as permanent!?) and the idea of sharing a roof had a lot to recommend it. The rest is history.

I have described earlier how we came to buy the first shared house, and some of the benefits we had anticipated, and a few of the disadvantages we hadn't thought of! The real surprises have been in the unexpected spin-offs, the ways in which sharing a house have enhanced my life in retirement. I had quite forgotten how good it is to have built-in encouragement. Of course, other friends can be helpful and encouraging, but being able to tap into instant feedback, be it for comment on an article, trying out an idea for a course, or do I look too fat in these trousers, all these add a dimension to my life which I'd never really expected to enjoy again.

More importantly for me has been the fact that, for the almost the first time I have shown my poetry to other people, and gained the courage to enter some of the poems in competitions. Quiet encouragement and constructive criticism are things we can and do offer to each other. I try out tricky bits of courses on the others, discuss difficulties with the tutoring sometimes. I can beat my head against the wall over a tricky bit of writing and know that someone will almost certainly silently hand me the cup of coffee or the glass of wine.

As a non-driver I appreciate the extra freedom that having two cars in the 'family' has given me. For instance, today, jaded by too much hunching over the computer, I was whisked to the sea to enjoy the sun and air for an hour (mind you, they chained me to it again when we came back!) and this I really value. I can, and still do, get myself to places by public transport – one of my reasons for choosing to live here was that there is access to so many lovely places - but joint excursions are fun and can be much more spontaneous when you meet over breakfast and can decide that today's the day to take off somewhere. Similarly, the impulse to eat out doesn't have to be a matter of telephoning around hoping somebody's free – there's a fair chance that someone else will be happy to go.

Finally not least of the ways in which sharing a house has enhanced my retirement has been the pleasure of living in such a lovely house, something I couldn't even have begun to think of buying on my own. We have spacious rooms, a pleasant outlook and just about enough garden to keep us happy. Of course, life isn't always a bed of roses. We do have our 'off' moments but who doesn't? On the whole retirement is giving me an interesting and stimulating life in ways I couldn't possibly have imagined ten years ago. Who knows what the next ten years will bring!

Retirement for beginners
Greta's tale

As the youngest and most recently retired member of the household I have obviously been giving some thought to how I wish to live in the future.

I am fortunate in that I come from a long-lived healthy family, so, in theory, I could still have at least a third of my life yet to live. This is a comforting thought and the decisions do not have to be hurried. For the present it is a delight to wake each morning in the knowledge that I can structure the day as I wish. So what have I done so far and what choices have I considered and tried out?

At first, like many of retired people I went on a few holidays. While these were looked forward to and much enjoyed I have no wish to continue with this on a regular basis. I made many assumptions about what I would like to do, most of these were based on the kinds of 'escape' activities which brought much pleasure when fitted into the hectic role of full-time employee, daughter, wife and mother.

Walking, particularly in Cumbria and North Yorkshire, has always been one of my passions. During my working life I would aim to walk in the hills two or three times a month. I assumed I would do this more often once I had retired. Not so! I still walk, but certainly no more than before. I find the mountain tops are not as important as they recently were. I now savour the pleasures to be found in the gentle walks through woodland and valley and along lake sides and streams. I take much more notice of my surroundings and love to capture a scene with my camera.

Photography has long been an enthusiasm. I now have the time, if not the money, to spend. It pleases me to record people and places for myself and sometimes for others. At the moment I am learning the techniques of the darkroom which introduces another dimension.

One of my best decisions came about almost by accident. After talking to a very keen archaeologist on a local walk I decided to enrol on a forty week course. I had no idea what to expect, but have found a fascinating new interest which I feel will stay with me for the rest of my life. I have been on field trips to the Orkneys and the south of England, completed course work, and will sit an exam in six weeks time. I have made new friends, learned new skills and a lot of information about the human past, for 99% of which archaeology is the only source of information.

"Claims she found it all by herself!"

How does sharing a house influence or help in making decisions about the future? I have always found the support of women friends a source of sustenance. How convenient to have them 'on tap'!

One example of how this can work is when one of us mentioned she would love to visit an art exhibition in a nearby town. I remembered reading of a Bronze Age exhibition in a museum in the same town and suggested we went together. We visited the two very different exhibitions together and over lunch discussed how much we had enjoyed both. We picked up leaflets of other exhibitions and events we might go to, including one about the archaeological exhibition *Early*

People which is in the New Museum of Scotland in Edinburgh. Last week I took my mother to see this and we both enjoyed it very much. The new information gained from these two exhibitions has since augmented my archaeological project.

So, have I reached any major decisions about how I wish to live my life from now on, or am I still a beginner? The answer is that I am not sure. I feel I have made some good and satisfying choices, but in a few years time, who knows? Making choices is both important and necessary, if we are to have any direction. But choices, unlike puppies, are not for life. Situations can change which make earlier choices less relevant. New directions will need to be determined. Perhaps in this sense we are all beginners.

Sharing a House Keeps us Healthy

As an ex-Health Promotion specialist, It has fallen to me to write this section about how we feel about our health, and our attempts to maintain it. Health is quite a difficult thing to define, as it tends to mean different things to different people. For some, being healthy might mean never having to go to the doctor, for others it might mean eating the 'right food.' For others it may be the ability to live life to the full, or to feel happy most of the time. Even those with the same chronic illness may differ in terms of how this is experienced. One will 'suffer' it, while another will 'manage' it and even enjoy a good quality of life.

When we made the decision to share a house, we were obviously thinking quite long term. When one is embarking on this kind of project, one becomes very future oriented. Of course we all feel we would like to stay fit and well, into our nineties, and while we are realistic enough to know that this may not be possible, we would like to improve our chances of achieving this by taking control of our health. We have all looked at making life-style changes, some of these are shared while others are individual.

On the whole we are all fairly healthy. Of course we suffer from a few of the illnesses of later years. We have our fair share of sciatica, back, knee and joint problems, but we like to feel we can find ways of coping with these things, without resorting to too many pills and potions. We visit our different doctors when the need arises, and we have all used complementary therapists from time to time; notably a reflexologist, osteopath, chiropractor, reiki practitioner, and a medical herbalist, and have found most to be very helpful. We also attend tai-chi classes, which we all find very beneficial for our mental health, relaxation and flexibility. Being able to afford these when needed, is one of the benefits of cutting down on expenses by sharing a house.

Other things that can be afforded such as a good hair dresser, the odd night out, the bottle of wine, can give a boost to our mental health by the feel-good factor. Between us we possess a number of DIY skills, but on occasion have to admit defeat and call in the experts. The ability to afford this is another bonus. Similarly we can all do housework (of course we can, we are women) but we also pay a cleaner to come in once every two weeks so we don't have to do all of it, thus conserving our energies for other more rewarding things. It has often been said that laughter is the best medicine. We certainly laugh a lot in this house.

We eat very healthily on the whole, eating foods which we know are good for us (together with the occasional 'treat'- we are not saints.) Our regular diet consists of fruit, vegetables and salads, (organic where possible) with a small amount of fish, beans, lentils, rice, pasta, cereals and good bread. We are aware of nutrients and herbs that can be helpful, and take supplements occasionally, but not all the time. We keep moving, walking the dog, swimming, rambling, tai-chi, gardening and cycling, are some of the activities carried out. Walking into town or to the shops has the added benefit of saving money on petrol or bus fares. We keep ourselves mentally active too, reading, keeping up with the news and with local events, attending adult education courses and U3A classes. Doing different things with different people and friends outside the house means that the three of us have lots to talk about whenever we get together. Of course most of these things could be done while living alone, but it might be easier to just slump in front of the television with a snack.

Just after Christmas this year, we all succumbed to a virus, luckily, not all at once, so we were able to look after each other, ensuring the shopping was done, medication was obtained, meals were cooked and so on. This was clearly of great benefit to us all. While we willingly give and receive short term care of this sort, we are not into caring on a long term basis. If one, or more of us becomes incapacitated through chronic illness, care can be bought in. Should health deteriorate further then, in agreement with the person involved and her family, the best available residential care will be sought. This has all been agreed in advance on the advice of our solicitor and is written into our Trust Deed. We will tackle future health problems as and when they arise, and acknowledge that we may have to make separate provision for living at some point. In the meantime we continue to look forward to sharing as many years of good quality health as possible.

POSTSCRIPT

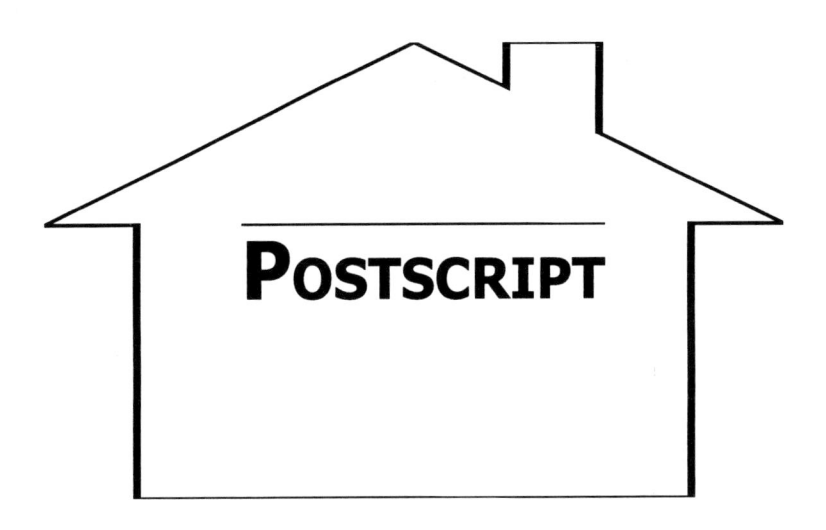

More and more we are finding that matrilocal* families including grandmother-figures and aunt-figures have established themselves from the fall-out of the nuclear family. Such segregated communities may hold great advantages for women and children, especially if they can find ways of incorporating older women who are now the majority of the elderly living alone on benefit. Governments could encourage a more rational use of housing stock and more caring in society by taxing households containing more than one occupant less than households with a single occupant, in diametric opposition to the British poll or council tax system. Whereas tax allowances to heterosexual couples clearly advantage one way of life over another, a household tax allowance would privilege all co-habitation systems, straight and gay, including the several-women-with-children unit. This would make sense in fiscal terms because people living in groups can take care of each other and should require less intervention than sole occupants with no one at home

> *to help if they meet with illness or accident. It might also mitigate the grim architectural consequences of a predominance of single-occupancy housing units. The family is dead, long live the family. The word 'family' actually means not kin-group but household. Maybe, instead of dating services, we should set up household-formation services to help like-minded individuals to set up house together.*

Germaine Greer – *The Whole Woman* (p329) [1]

We have quoted this passage at some length because it seems to underline some of the points we have been making. Of course, like all seminal thinkers Greer can overstate the case on occasion, but so often in the past she has predicted the trends in society and urged women to act upon them. One does not have to be a militant feminist to appreciate the validity of much of what she says, and to see that the new millennium will inevitably see considerable changes in the way we all live our lives.

Whether we should actually penalise people who choose to live alone is a moot point. There should, surely, always be choices. Also, as we discovered, the need for personal, identifiable space is very strong. It is fine to idealise the idea of group-living provided that none of the group is exploited. There is just a small worry that bringing in grandmother and aunt-figures might be seen as an easy way to deal with the child care problem!

> * Chamber's defines matrilocal as '*a form of marriage in which the husband goes to live with the wife's family*'. We assume that Greer is using the term to infer that there are now many women returning to, or perhaps not leaving, the maternal home.

Rather like having a new puppy, and finding that you notice far more dogs than ever before, we are increasingly aware of how much shared living is going on out there. We have given some examples of these in our section – Options. There are, and have been, many societies in which group living is the norm; not all of them exclude men. Indeed, one of the questions that has been raised with us is whether or not we have come across examples of men setting up shared living groups. The answer is no, although there are instances of mixed groups both in the USA and the Netherlands.

Nevertheless, the trends are there. Society is changing. Many of the new generation of older women have far greater aspirations and a clearer view of what they want than their mothers and grandmothers. Life does not end at retirement; we don't have to retreat behind the net curtains. As one of us has said earlier, we could have a third of our lives left to live and, like most women, for a lot of our lives we have all accommodated to families, partners, jobs, social pressures. We have made choices; but the range of choice was limited by circumstances.

We three have been able to determine our new direction; demands on us have reduced. We are very fortunate. On the other hand, as Pasteur suggested, we have cultivated prepared minds and fortune has favoured us. We were alert to the possibilities of different modes of living, seized our opportunity and were prepared to take chances. We see our shared living as part of the positive move towards offering more choice, both financial and social, to older women who don't wish to be bound by the stereotypes of the past. Of course, we realise that not all women are able or, indeed, wish to do what we have done, but we like to feel that we are part of a growing trend in which women generally are enabled to see that retirement can be a new beginning, and is a new venture.

To take but one example, all of us have chosen to pursue new learning challenges. Learning for its own sake is very much a preferred option for a lot of women, be it astrology or zoology - art or yoga! There's so much out there to do. U3A has been important for two of us, and the three of us actually met through an Older Women's Network. Also, *Growing Old Disgracefully* [2], through its publications and newsletter network, has done much to shift the stereotypes, and help to portray older women as interesting and dynamic people. We are entitled to choice, and it doesn't have to be the full grandmother role – all the time. We have to learn that it's OK for grandma to say, 'Sorry, next Wednesday I'm busy, it's my philosophy class, and on Friday I go to Tai Chi'. It is now more acceptable for women generally to express their needs, and to spend time giving consideration to the practical ways in which they can enhance their lives.

Of course, our earlier discussions were centred mainly around the practical, although our joint membership of such organisations as U3A and the Older Women's Network indicated that we were of like minds. It's the discussions round the kitchen table that have made clear how much basic philosophy we share. Sorting out the books really gave the game away - the duplication of titles and writers was amazing. There they all were, the 'greats' - Germaine Greer, Betty Friedan, Mary Stott, Katherine Whitehorn, Alice Walker, Maya Angelou etc. The list is long (some of them appear in the book list in Appendix C) These women have influenced us, even when we don't always agree with them! What they have done is to show that women do have choices, they do have the right to some control over their own lives.

One criticism which has arisen is that in living in a group we actually give up some personal control. Of course, there is some truth in this but the fact remains that this particular 'experiment' will probably last as long as we all feel that we are gaining more than we are losing. We have explored a lot of both the 'ups' and the 'downs'; we have tried to be honest! We have had some stern criticism to deal with and have felt our strength as a group in dealing with it.

It has been suggested that one advantage could be that there is constant stimulus of ideas and activities. We were intrigued by this perception as we see ourselves as quite often helping each other to 'waste' time, but the suggestion certainly precipitated a lot of discussion. On the whole, we decided that in the initial stages when the group is coalescing it is probably true - there is an explosion of ideas to be shared and explored. However, as the group stabilises and acquires more shared experience there is the danger of stagnation. Groups can choose to implode, explode or evolve. We hope we are evolving. This is when the maintenance of a full external life for each individual becomes important, so that fresh experiences are fed back into the group. As to wasting time, we have decided that if we can't indulge in interesting discussion and a lot of laughter at this stage in our lives we've somehow got it wrong! And of course there are times when talking is a marvellous way of putting something off!

Naturally we put on a good show for occasions – who doesn't? Sometimes daily life is very mundane, people get irritable - who doesn't? There are no short cuts, and no escaping from yourself; you bring all your 'baggage' with you into the situation. We have been reminded several times of the story of the two men who were moving to a new town. Outside the walls sat an old man. The first man approached and asked what the townsfolk were like. 'What were they like where you've come from?' 'Mean and unpleasant', replied the man. 'That's what you'll find here' replied the old man. The second man asked the same question. 'What were they like where you've come from?' ' Kind and helpful and always cheerful.' The old man nodded. 'That's exactly what they're like here'. It is vital to retain goodwill and to avoid malice. At one particularly low point the question of bringing the whole experiment to an end was seriously mooted. 'Well, of course' said one, 'we'll all have to help each other find somewhere else suitable to live'. There was silence, followed by gales of laughter. The triumph of goodwill over irritation!

In conclusion, if we recognise that there are always various currents of change in society, then what we are trying to do is to harness some of the flow and to direct our lives into the appropriate channel for ourselves, at this time in our lives. We hope that if this book does nothing else it will show that choices are not confined to the young, and that women of any age can make new beginnings and seize opportunities. Go for whatever you want, however small – or large!

Notes

(1) Germaine Greer *The Whole Woman* Doubleday 1999
(2) The Hen Coop *Growing Old Disgracefully* Piatkus 1992

APPENDIX A

The following questions are intended to raise what we feel are some of the most important points to consider if you are even half-seriously thinking of sharing a house. Where appropriate, we have put in page references of possibly helpful comments in the main text. As we suggested earlier (p 20) it might be a good idea to do this questionnaire twice, once before reading the book and then afterwards in the light of your reactions to it.

1) Do you know enough interested people to ensure that at least someone will want to go ahead, bearing in mind that a lot of people do drop out? (pp 23 - 24)

2) How much money can you afford for this venture? (pp 35 - 36) Bear in mind that you need to consider not only capital but ongoing expenses. Do you all agree on what you can afford separately and jointly?

3) What are your basic needs – size of house, special requirements, location, etc.?

(A joint check list is a good idea – p 38)

4) Do you have a solicitor interested and approving of your venture? Even the nicest can be very disapproving if it's outside their experience! We can only suggest asking around and interviewing one or two!

5) Are you willing/able to trust your group with the necessary details of your finances in order to set up the venture?

6) Could you deal sensitively with discrepancies in income?

(Tricky this one – see p 37 and p 58)

7) Are you prepared to be bound by a legal Trust Deed or similar legal arrangement?   (pp 41 - 42)

8) What aspirations do you have for your retirement? Is shared living going to help in the realisation of your goals? (See – *Personal Reflections – our own thoughts*)

9) Do you honestly believe that you have the necessary levels of tolerance and flexibility to survive the very necessary adjustments and compromises?

10) Do you see this idea as the end of the beginning or the beginning of the end?

(Serious question! cue for philosophical discussion!)

We hope that you will have come up with some more important questions of your own.

Good luck!

APPENDIX B

This short book list is by no means intended to be definitive! These are books and writers which have interested one or all of us.

de Beauvoir S.	*Old Age*	Penguin ('77) ('70)
Bown J.	*Women of Consequence*	Chatto & Windus('86)
Brenton M.	*Choice, Autonomy & mutual support*	Rowntree Foundation('99)
Brooke E.	*Women Healers thro' History*	Women's Press ('82)
Cameron & Charlesworth	*All That . . . the other half of History*	Pandora ('86)
Curtiss Z.	*Life after Work*	Women's Press ('99)
Ecker G. (ed.)	*Feminist Aesthetics*	Women's Press ('85)
Eisenstein H.	*Contemporary Feminist Thought*	Counterpoint ('84)
Friedan B.	*Fountain of Age*	Vintage ('94)
Greer G.	*The Whole Woman*	Doubleday ('99)
Griffin S.	*Women & Nature*	Women's Press ('84)

Hen Coop	*Growing Old Disgracefully* Piatkus ('92)
	Disgracefully Yours Piatkus ('95)
Hobby E.	*Virtue of Necessity* Virago ('88)
Kenner C.	*No Time for Women* Pandora ('85)
Murtz H. ed.	*When I'm an Old Woman I shall wear purple* Papier Mache ('91)
Payne K. ed.	*Between Ourselves* Picador ('83)
Phillips A. & Rakusen	*Our Bodies Ourselves* Penguin ('78)
Steinham G.	*Revolution from Within* Bloomsbury ('92)
Stott M.	*Ageing for Beginners* Penguin ('81)
Taylor A.	*Older than Time* Aquarian ('83)
Walker A.	*In Search of our Mothers' Gardens* Womens' Press ('84)
	Living by the Word Womens' Press ('88)
Wallace T.	*Two Old Women* Womens' Press ('84)
Woolf V.	*Women & Writing* Womens' Press ('79)
	A Room of One's Own Flamingo ('94)

Appendix C - Floor plans

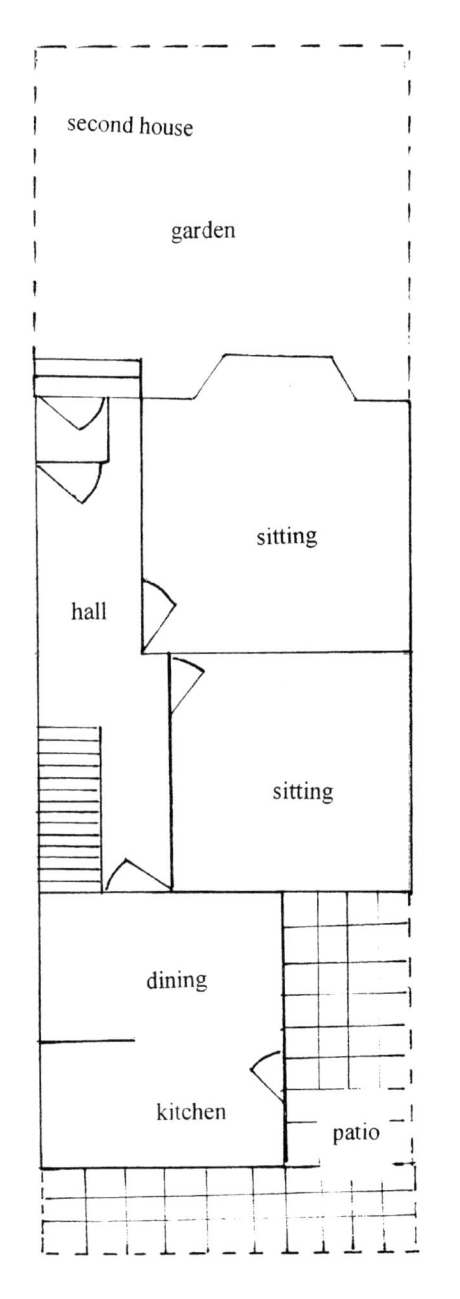

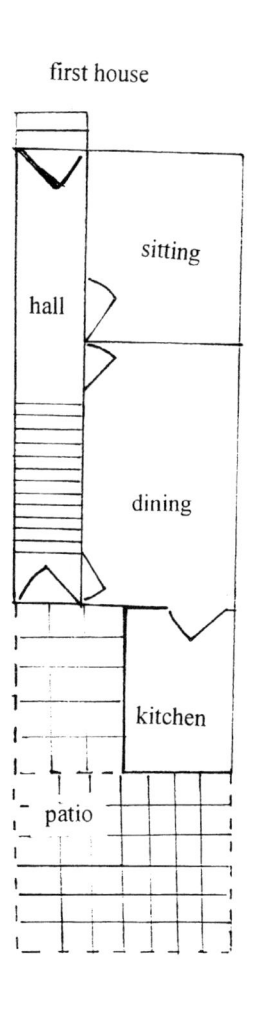

Useful contacts

Advice, Information and Mediation Service for Retirement Housing (AIMS)
(supported by **Age Concern**)
Walkden House
3-10 Melton Street
London NW1 2EJ
0171 383 2006

Age Concern England
1268 London Road
London SW16 4EJ
Information Line
0800 7314931

Age Concern Ireland
114-116 Pearse Street
Dublin 2 Ireland
+3531 677 9892

Age Concern Northern Ireland
3 Lower Crescent
Belfast BT7 1NR
01232 245 729

Age Concern Scotland
113 Rose Street
Edinburgh EH2 3DT
0131 220 3345

Age Concern Wales
1 Cathedral Road
Cardiff CF1 9SD
01222 371566

Association of Retired Persons Over 50 (ARPO50)
Greencoat House
Francis Place,
London SW1P 1DZ
0171 828 0500

Centre for Policy on Ageing
25-31 Ironmonger Row
London EC1V 3QP
0171 253 1787

Christian Council on Ageing
c/o Epworth House
Stuart Street
Derby
DE1 2EQ

Citizens Advice Bureaux Central Office
Myddleton House
115-123 Pentonville Road
N1 9LZ
0171 833 2181

An experiment in living

Counsel and Care for the Elderly
Twyman House
16 Bonny Street
London NW1 9PG
0171 485 1550/1566

CRUSE Bereavement Care
Cruse House
126 Sheen Road
Richmond
Surrey TW9 1UR
0181 940 4818/332 7227

The Disabled Living Centre
(for details of local Centres)
Winchester House
10 Cranmer Road
London SW9 6EJ
0171 820 0567

Disabled Living Foundation
380-384 Harrow Road
London W9 2HU
0171 289 6111

Elderly Accommodation Council
46 Chiswick High Road
London W4 1SZ
0181 742 1182

Growing Old Disgracefully Network,
103 Grosvenor Avenue,
Carshalton SM5 3EP

Help the Aged
St James's Walk
Clerkenwell Green
London EC1R 0BE
0171 253 0253
SeniorLine 0800 650065

Humanist Housing Association
Holmes Place
London NW5 3AA
0171 485 8776

Independent Housing Ombudsman Service
Norman House
105-109 Strand
London WC2R 0AA
0171 836 3630

The Law Society
113 Chancery Lane
London WC2A 1PL
0171 242 1222

Law Centres Federation
Duchess House
198-19 Warren Street
London W1P 5DB
0171 387 8570

National Housing Federation
175 Gray's Inn Road
London WC1X 8UP
0171 278 6571

National Institute of Adult Continuing Education (NIACE)
21 De Montford Street
Leicester LE1 7GE
0116 255 1451

Leasehold Advisory Service (LEASE)
6-8 Maddox Street
London W1R 9PN
0171 493 3116

National Association of Widows
54-57 Allison Street
Digbeth, Birmingham B5 5TH
0121 643 8348

National Council for the Divorced and Separated
PO Box 519
Leicester LE2 3ZE
0116 2700 595

Pre-Retirement Association (PRA)
9 Chesham Road
Guildford GU1 3LS
01483 301170

The Ramblers Association
1-5 Wandsworth Road
London SW8 2XX
0171 582 6878

The University of the Third Age (U3A)
26 Harrison Street
London WC1H 8JG
0171 837 8838

THIRD AGE PRESS
*. . . a unique publishing company
inspired by older people*

*. . . an independent
publishing company which recognizes that the
period of life after full-time employment and family
responsibility can be a time of fulfilment and
continuing development
. . . a time of regeneration*

Third Age Press

. . . books are available on order from good bookshops or by direct mail order to Third Age Press. All prices include UK p & p. Please add 20% for other countries.

UK Sterling cheques payable to *Third Age Press.*

**6 Parkside Gardens London SW19 5EY
Phone 0208 947 0401   Fax 0208 944 9316
e-mail: dnort@thirdagepress.co.uk
Website: www.thirdagepress.co.uk
Dianne Norton ~ Managing Editor**

Registered in England Company Number 2678599
VAT registered 627 9627 01

On the Tip of Your Tongue:
your memory in later life

by Dr H B Gibson . . . (a mere octogenarian himself) explores memory's history and examines what an 'ordinary' person can expect of their memory. He reveals the truth behind myths about memory and demonstrates how you can manage your large stock of memories and your life. Wittily illustrated by Rufus Segar.

Includes:

What is memory? The four memory systems. Different sorts of memory.

How is your memory changing? Meeting people. Mistaking physical for mental change. Remembering to do things.

The 'Tip-of-the-tongue' phenomenon - Breaking the blockage. The puzzle of blocked recall. The Freudian explanation.

Gimmicks for remembering: Mnemonics - Place method - Pegwords - learning foreign words - 'chunking' - list of memory aids.

Improving your memory - Memory training. A practical training course. What kind of memory have you got?

Will you continue to make progress all your life? Memory at different stages of life. Enemies of progress. Reminiscence.

Derangements, diseases and injuries that effect memory. Brain damage, amnesia, depression, senility, Alzheimer-type conditions.   **1995 160pages   ISBN 1 898576 05X £7.00**

Buy this book together with *A little of what you fancy* for only £13.00

A Little of What You Fancy Does You Good: your health in later life

by Dr H B Gibson ~ illustrated by Rufus Segar

'Managing an older body is like running a very old car - as the years go by you get to know its tricks and how to get the best out of it, so that you may keep it running sweetly for years and years' . . . so says Dr H B Gibson in his sensible and practical book which respects your intelligence and, above all, appreciates the need to enjoy later life. It explains the whys, hows and wherefores of exercise, diet and sex ~ discusses 'You and your doctor' and deals with some of the pitfalls and disabilities of later life. But the overall message is positive and Rufus Segar's illustrations once again bring whimsy and insight to a very readable text. Dr H B Gibson gives due cause for optimism.

Includes:

How much exercise do you take? - Determinants of fitness. How fitness can be regained in later life.

What about diet? - The constituents of food. Miraculous food & food additives. Can diet increase your life span?

What about sex? Myths about sex in later life. What sexuality means in later life. Shyness.

You and your doctor - Different types of patients. The doctors' dilemmas with older patients.

Some pitfalls in later life - Eating - drinking - smoking. Personality types.

Disability in later life - phyical conditions, sensory loss, dementias, depression, bereavement, loneliness etc.

1997   256 pages   ISBN 1 898576   £8.50

Consider the Alternatives: healthy strategies for later life
by Dr Caroline Lindsay Nash
Illustrated by Maggie Guillon

This book offers a clear and unbiased explanation of the nature and uses of a wide range of alternative therapies... what you can expect of complementary medicine... and why yoga, pets, music and humour can contribute to your personal strategy for a healthy thirdage. There are also contributions from Dr Michael Lloyd, a psychologist specialising in the management of pain, and from pensioner, Tony Carter, on how and why he thinks you should take control of your own health.

Maggie Guillon's cartoons add a delightful touch.

Includes:
- *Alternative techniques of diagnosis*
- *Physical therapies - external body* - Back pain, chiropractic, cranio-sacral, physiotherapy, acupuncture, zero-balancing, Alexander technique
- *Physical therapies - internal body* - Nutrition, macrobiotics, herbalism, colonic irrigation
- *Mind over matter* - Psychoanalysis, psychodynamic counselling, humanistic approaches, psychosynthesis, counselling, group therapy, family therapy, transactional analysis, hypnotherapy
- *Something for the spirit* - Past life therapy, meditation, spiritual counselling, spiritual healing, reiki, psychics and mediums
- *A holistic view of health* - Homoeopathy, anthroposophical medicine, traditional Chinese medicine, Ayurveda
- *Exercise and relaxation* - Exercise, dance, yoga, tai chi, massage, tragerwork, shiatsu, aromatherapy, pets
- *The strange, rare and fun* - Flower remedies, crystal healing, colour therapy, feng shui, drama, art and music therapy, laughter

1998 160pages ISBN 1 898576 11 4 £7.00

Changes and Challenges in Later Life: learning from experience

Edited by Yvonne Craig
Foreword by Claire Rayner ~
illustrated by Maggie Guillon

Older people share with those of all ages the desire for fulfilment - a need to transform surviving into thriving. This book brings together experts from Britain's major caring organisations to share their wealth of experience and practical advice on the sometimes difficult situations of later life. The wealth of experience concentrated in this book shows how changes and challenges can lead to positive attitudes and action.

Contents and authors
- *Legal rights and remedies* **Barbara Beaton**, Age Concern Legal Unit
- *Neighbours* **Yvonne Joan Craig**, Elder Mediation Project of Mediation UK & **Archana Srivastava**, Stirling University
- *A good ending* **Gillian Dalley**, Centre for Policy on Ageing
- *Mistreatment and neglect* **Frank Glendenning**, Centre for Social Gerontology, Keele University
- *Making the most of change* **Mervyn Kohler**, Help the Aged
- *Who cares?* **Jill Pitkeathley**, Carers National Association
- *The right retirement home* **Rudi Reeves**, Advisory, Information & Mediation Service for Retirement Housing
- *Care homes, residents and relatives* **Jenny Stiles**, The Relatives Association

Maggie Guillon's drawings give a humourous perspective to each chapter.

1997 160pages ISBN 1 898576 10 6 £7.00